# THE GOLDEN CITY

HENRY HOPE REED, Jr.

# THE GOLDEN CITY

1959
DOUBLEDAY & COMPANY, INC.
GARDEN CITY, NEW YORK

# ACKNOWLEDGMENTS

Grateful acknowledgment for permission to reprint passages is made to:

CHAPTER TWO
*Time* for selection from "More than Modern," article on Edward D. Stone, Vol. 71 (1958), No. 13, p. 64

CHAPTER THREE
Princeton University Press for passages in the *Papers* of Thomas Jefferson, Julian P. Boyd, editor (Princeton. N. J., 1954), Vol. 9, pp. 226, 227
Houghton Mifflin Company for selections from Henry Adams, *The Education of Henry Adams* (Boston, 1918), pp. 339, 340, 343; same for the selection from Charles Moore, *The Life and Times of Charles Follen McKim* (Boston, 1929), p. 303

CHAPTER FOUR
Doubleday & Co., for the passage from Geoffrey Scott, *The Architecture of Humanism* (New York, 1956), p. 171
Princeton University Press for a passage from *opus* cited, Vol. 8 (1953), p. 534
Charles Scribner's Sons for selection from Henry James, *A Small Boy and Others* (New York, 1913), pp. 345–47
Josiah Royce for the selection from Josiah Royce, *Race Questions, Provincialism and Other American Problems.* (The MacMillan Company, New York, 1908), p. 108

APPENDIX
G. P. Putnam's Sons for selections from John Lloyd Wright, *My Father Who Is on Earth* (New York, 1946), pp. 32, 33, 69

*For*
*Jenny Reed*
*and*
*Hebe Dick*

# Contents

# Foreword

THE ORIGIN of this book goes back fifteen years or so when the author first began to see America's past of wood, brick, and stone. The curiosity was there, nurtured by generous parents, and interest grew with time encouraged by trips of exploration in the company of two friends, Wayne Andrews and Alan Burnham. At the time the Modern was part of the enthusiasm—"it was of our time"—and did not conflict with the love of the past, but the enthusiasm was made uneasy by the Modernists' eagerness to obscure our heritage. Inevitably the work of other generations, notably that of the American Renaissance, began to appear superior in every way to the present and the Modern was questioned.

A sojourn in Europe only confirmed the prejudice. Walks in Rome in the footsteps of Augustus J. C. Hare opened new vistas and the sight-seeing was made easier by James Barber, of the British Council, and Signora Romoli, architect to Prince Doria Pamphily. In Florence the same exploration took place. In Venice there was the company of Guido Lorenzetti's *Venezia e il suo estuario* with special assistance from the late Nino Barbantini.

In Paris it took the form of attending, whenever possible, *visites-conférences* in staid mansions, government buildings, and royal palaces. The author had the good fortune to attend the École du Louvre, where the late Charles Mauricheau-Beaupré, director of the National Museum at Versailles, and Pierre Verlet, curator of objects of art at the Louvre, only raised the curtain higher on the wonders of the past. The beauty of the French capital was matched for him by the unfailing courtesy present in the form of encouragement to see the best. José Corti, Jean Landais, Denise Mayer, Georges Cattaui, Paul Tournon, and Albert Laprade helped the pilgrim on his journey, and many kind hands opened doors of houses and chateaux or pointed the way to gardens.

On the return home the past was there in thicker detail; much that had gone unnoticed now came into full view. It is obvious that only by knowing Europe well can the American possibly appreciate his country's best. The names of Thomas Jefferson, of Charles Follen McKim, of Whitney Warren and of Richard Morris Hunt, to name but a few, took on a value they had never held before. What quality did they have which was denied us? The answer was the classical image,

9

a fact brought home as nothing else by *Ars in Urbe,* an exhibition of civic art in the Yale University Art Gallery organized in 1953 by the then director, Lamont Moore, and by Christopher Tunnard, professor of city planning. It was so far ahead of its time in comprehension and purpose that it was not until after several years that its full meaning dawned: That the classical image is a living force still to be reckoned with, particularly in America. The object of this book is to show the worth of that force.

Several portions of the work, in different form, have already appeared in *Harper's* magazine, the New York *Times Magazine, Thought, National Sculpture Review, Journal* of the American Institute of Architects, *New World Writing,* and *Liturgical Arts.*

There is the special debt to the courteous staff of the Art Room of the New York Public Library, Ina Cassirer, Norwood Vail, Anthony Cardillo, Neal Richmond, Margaret Viviano, Namo S. Street, Takato Saito, Jane Waite, and to the assistant librarian of Avery Library, Columbia University, Adolph Placzek.

The author is also indebted, for information, encouragement, and counsel, to Elizabeth Fuller, Mrs. Louis Ayres, John O'Connor, William Adams Delano, Victor Weybright, Walter Knight Sturges, J. Sanford Shanley, Jr., Mme. Heuse-Coutan, Louis A. Simon, Samuel Wilson, Jr., Ruth Rubinstein, E. Powis Jones, Charles K. Warner, Arabel Porter, Patricia Gwynne, Ronald H. Pearce, Jerome D. Greene, and Theodore Bolton. For assistance in getting photographs thanks are due W. A. Probst of the Cunard Line, Nancy W. Boone of the Art Institute of Chicago, Dr. Hans Kronhubr of the Austrian Information Service, Ennio Valente of the Ente provinciale per il Turismo di Vicenza, and the late B. S. Boggis of Duveen Brothers.

The author is specially grateful to Wayne Andrews, John Barrington Bayley, Frederic Rhinelander King, and Richard Koch for the use of their photographs. Those of Wayne Andrews and John Barrington Bayley, as well as the author's, were developed and printed under the careful supervision of Richard J. Schuler of Compo Photo Service. To Joan Bartlett Reed he is obliged for the drawing of the "tree of Picturesque Secessionism," to Mrs. Lyda Nelson of the Architects Emergency Committee for the words of Cass Gilbert quoted in Chapter Four. The author is particularly indebted to Robert T. Vanderbilt, Jr., who warned him that the countryside must not be forgotten.

Rollin Jensen, Arthur Upham Pope, Serge Hughes, and Walter Webb Reed read portions of the manuscript and the author is grateful for their suggestions.

Christopher Tunnard showed the way and John Barrington Bayley was guide to the project.

Above all, the author is under particular obligation to Clark McLain for comments and ideas.

The uncredited photographs must be put down to the account of the author.

# THE GOLDEN CITY

# CHAPTER ONE

# The City of Contrasts

A CURIOUS change is taking place in the American scene. For the first time since towns and cities began to rise in the land, buildings and other improvements are appearing consciously designed without ornament. Where once the street was crowded with sculptured detail we are now being offered a wasteland. Where once towers graced the skyline, slabs now obstruct it. Nothing seems to escape the giant vacuum cleaner of fashion as it passes over our communities, robbing them of all embellishment. The change is an obvious sign of a larger power, the superstition of the Modern, and the comparison which follows is only an introduction to that power.

The City of Contrasts consists of pictures of similar building types and objects placed opposite each other. On the left-hand side the reader will find a decorated building or flagpole base—with few exceptions they date from a generation or so ago—on the right-hand side a barren one of today. Each one is identified as to date and architect, and a description is offered as well. The work of the leading men has been selected to give substance to the comparison. Let the reader take a look at the City of Contrasts and judge for himself if the change has been for the better. While the majority of the examples are to be found in New York City, any American community will furnish them for the curious.

A word of caution to the reader. The buildings and objects are here presented in photographs. To judge works of art through the camera's eye is to fall into error. The photograph, as useful as it is, cannot convey depth, detail, or true color. (In the matter of color, color transparencies or colored positives are notoriously deceiving.) With its two-dimensional quality it flatters the abstract element of any object, and more than one contemporary architect and designer has known success thanks to the camera's distortion. It cannot reveal the full measure of beauty of a work of art, particularly great architectural compositions. The reader is urged to see with his own eyes the buildings and objects shown here, or their equivalent, wherever he lives. Another America will come into his view.

*Main façade of the Metropolitan Museum of Art at Fifth Avenue and Eighty-second Street. Designed in 1894 by Richard Morris Hunt and Richard Howland Hunt. The sculpture is by Karl Bitter. (J. B. Bayley)*

The first story consists of a high rusticated base. Three wide bays with round arches are separated by four sets of twin Corinthian columns; between each pair there is an empty niche and a plaque bordered with elaborate molding. The bays on either side of the entrance bay have two small columns inserted and a rusticated wall carrying a simple entablature, while above come the windows. In the central bay the columns and rusticated wall give way to an entrance. Helmeted masks adorn the keystones of the bays, and the spandrels have relief portraits set in round frames. An elaborate broken cornice tops the whole, bearing four large uncarved blocks of stone; when carved, they will be trophies. Behind them is an attic with a cornice and antefixae of female masks joined together by fruit swags. The steps, it must be noted, are essential to the monumental effect. If they are removed, the façade will become as a man's face without a lower jaw.

*Rendering of the new museum of the Solomon R. Guggenheim Foundation, designed by Frank Lloyd Wright, now being completed on Fifth Avenue between Eighty-eighth and Eighty-nine streets. To be finished in 1958. (Drawn by Robert Galster)*

The construction exemplifies the principle of steel and concrete in tension. The architect has said: "The consequent cantilever and the science of continuity appear in consistent form as a complete building in which to view the art this organic building was designed to reward and reveal." The decoration will consist of trees, shrubs, and vines.

*Head of the cast-iron lamppost still to be found on the streets of New York City. Designed under the supervision of Richard Rodgers Bowker when vice-president of the Edison Electric Illuminating Company. Initial design in 1892, final design in 1896.*

The famous bishop's-crook lamppost of New York City springs from a capital adorned with acanthus leaves. Elaborate tendrils curve to center in a rosette. The tendrils are bound to the lamp loop by a sheath of acanthus leaves. It is a popular symbol of classical New York. Richard Rodgers Bowker, the man responsible for the design, enjoyed an unusual career in business and in civic life; one of his many interests was the magazine, *Publishers' Weekly,* of which he was founder and owner.

*Head of the new stainless-steel lamppost to be found on Park Row near the City Hall. Designed in 1956 by the Department of Water Supply, Gas and Electricity, city of New York.*

A tapering pole of stainless steel rises to an arm which projects at about a 120° angle. An excellent example of form following function.

*Main façade of the Grand Central Terminal. Designed in 1910 by Whitney Warren. Mercury and reclining figures by Jules Coutan.*

A low first story, concealed by the ramp, carries the main portion of the façade. Three tall, wide window bays (bays of this size are peculiar to America) are divided by high bases from which rise two pairs of fluted shafts with Roman Doric capitals, the pairs in turn separated by windows. An elaborate entablature has as its central feature a broken round pediment, with a clock insert, which supports a colossal Mercury and two reclining figures. Swags and garlands of fruit, laurel wreaths, and voluted keystones decorate various parts of the façade. Below the central pediment stands the bronze statue of the frock-coated Commodore Cornelius Vanderbilt by A. de Groot.

*Main façade of the Bus Terminal of the Port of New York Authority on Eighth Avenue and Fortieth Street, designed in 1948 and completed in 1950 by the Port Authority Engineering Department.*

One of the largest bus terminals in the world and the entrance to a great city, it offers a large front of brick and stone trim. There is no sculpture, no sculptural detail, and no ornament of any kind outside and none inside.

*Old wing of the Yale University Art Gallery. Designed in 1928 by Egerton Swartout.*

The architect was inspired by the Romanesque and Gothic of Northern Italy. Windows of mullions and tracery are set in deep, round-arched bays crowned by dripstones. In the tower, a portion of which is seen at the right, the tracery consists of two cinquefoil arches with a four-cusped circle, while the wall above the door is broken by a traceried window with a balcony. Above the windows of the wing are fixed sculptured panels and one cut-rolled-leather shield, the whole topped by an elaborate cornice and an attic.

*New wing of the Yale University Art Gallery. Designed in 1953 by Louis I. Kahn.*

A sixty-foot wall of yellow brick, broken by four horizontal lines of flat stone, faces the street. A glass wall set at a right angle to the brick wall rises above the entrance.

*Brooklyn Heights Branch of the Manufacturers Trust Company at 177 Montague Street, Brooklyn. Designed in 1915 by Edward Palmer York and Philip Sawyer. (J. B. Bayley)*

The façade is divided into two parts, the bottom half consisting of a high rusticated base of vermiculated limestone, with a coursing separating the first story and a mezzanine. The top half has monumental engaged columns and pilasters of the Corinthian order rising two stories, with the lower story having balustrades. Above, a simple entablature with a wide cornice crowns the whole. A Vitruvian scroll separates the two halves of the façade. The rusticated base conveys a sense of power by its height and detail, the columns and pilasters above a sense of restrained grandeur.

*Fifth Avenue Branch of the Manufacturers Trust Company at 510 Fifth Avenue.*
*Designed in 1955 by Gordon Bunshaft of Skidmore, Owings & Merrill.*

A glass front is broken into rectangles by stainless-steel trim. Colored glass is used in the spandrels of the upper stories to emphasize the angular abstract pattern. Instead of ornament the glass affords a view of the interior, where rows of flowers or bushes, changed seasonally, are found on the first and second stories. The first story, in addition, offers a view of a large open safe and the side of an escalator.

*Bronze lintel above the first-story window of the Postum Building at 250 Park Avenue, designed in 1924 by Cross & Cross, with Phelps Barnum, associate.*

A Medusa is set against a ground of imbricated leaves within a bowl ornamented by a cable molding. Bay-leaf branches edge the bowl, and the whole is placed on a crisscross of squares filled with rosettes bordered by a leaf-and-dart molding.

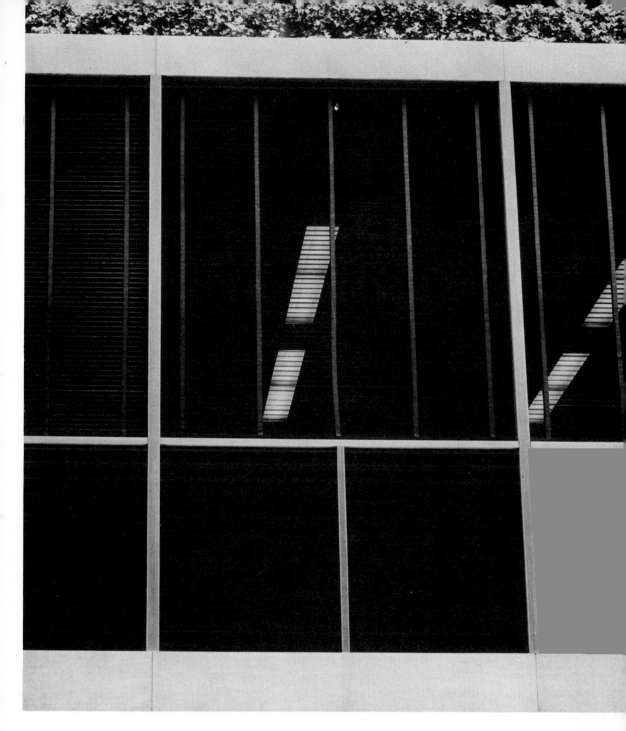

*Glass lintel above the first story of Lever House, 390 Park Avenue. Designed in 1952 by Gordon Bunshaft of Skidmore, Owings & Merrill.*

No comment.

*Soldiers and Sailors Memorial Arch in the Grand Army Plaza, Brooklyn. Designed in 1889 by John H. Duncan and dedicated in 1892. The heroic groups are by Frederick W. MacMonnies. The bas-reliefs are by Maurice J. Power. The spandrel figures are by Philip Martiny. Inside the piers of the arch are two bronze reliefs, one of Lincoln and the other of Grant, both by Thomas Eakins and William R. O'Donovan. (J. B. Bayley)*

A single arch with two piers and a simple entablature. It serves to carry clustered groups, soldiers on the left and sailors on the right, being led by armed, winged female figures. Above the arch Victory rides a two-horse chariot, carrying a sword in one hand and a signum in the other. Winged figures leading horses and blowing trumpets walk beside her.

*Metal arch, 590 feet high, for the Jefferson Memorial Park in St. Louis, Missouri. Designed in 1947–48 by Saarinen, Saarinen & Associates. As yet unbuilt. (Hendrich-Blessing Studio, courtesy Jefferson National Expansion Memorial)*

No comment.

*Water god above the entrance of the Chase Manhattan Company at 40 Wall Street by the sculptor Eli Nadelman 1929. H. Craig Severance, architect, with Yasuo Matsui, associate.*

The sculptor, better known for his Modern original work, here bows to a classical precedent. One of the institutions which joined to form the present one had its origin in a water company, and the artist adopted the ancient figure of the river god to symbolize its past.

*"Continuum" by José de Rivera, 1956, decorating the entrance of 711 Third Avenue. William Lescaze, architect.*

The above abstraction of stainless steel, nine feet three inches wide, is explained by the artist as follows: "Themes and symbols are no longer valid for the new architecture . . . The beauty and source of excitement in this work is found in the interdependence and relationship of the form . . . My idea was to integrate a form with a wall; to provide pleasurable animation for the area."

*The Diego Suarez residence on Long Island. Designed in 1953 by Frederic Rhine-lander King of Wyeth & King. Garden designed by Diego Suarez. (F. R. King)*

A rare example of a Palladian villa built since World War II. Set in a formal garden with pools, fountains, statues, and clipped trees, the house is of white-painted brick. On the garden front, of which this is a view, two windows and a central door look out from a large salon. Above the windows are round niches with busts set on volutes, also serving as keystones. Over the door is an elaborate foliage ornament. Above the cornice is a low attic on which stand four statues. Urns ornament the wings.

*Falling Water, the Edgar K. Kaufmann residence, Bear Run, Pennsylvania. Designed in 1936 by Frank Lloyd Wright. (Wayne Andrews)*

A large split-level house of rough stone and concrete is cantilevered over a stream in the woods of western Pennsylvania.

*Office building at the corner of Leonard Street and Broadway dating from the 1860's. (J. B. Bayley)*

A cast-iron building with Renaissance detail. The present second story has Corinthian pilasters and engaged columns. Quoins distinguish the corners of the structure, while on top a cornice is supported at intervals by voluted brackets.

*The Socony-Mobil Building at Forty-second Street and Lexington Avenue. Designed in 1955 by Harrison & Abramovitz. (J. B. Bayley)*

A slab, the building has walls of steel, gray gun metal in color, and marked with a triangular geometric pattern. The windows are sealed because the building is entirely air-conditioned. The bottom portion has a revetment of blue glass set in steel trim.

*The former Edward S. Beyer residence at 32 East Seventieth Street. Designed in 1912
by Alfredo Taylor and Julian Clarence Levi.*

A good example of the private house of the 1900's which was a New York
specialty. The entrance is distinguished by three stone posts holding vases with
garlands of fruit and pine cones set in acanthus leaves. The doorway and window
are round-arched with ornamental molding and keystones. The high second-story
windows have balustraded balconies and pediments supported on voluted brackets.
Above, the third-story windows are bordered by large volutes rising to small volutes at the top. A fourth story has a balustraded terrace carried on brackets;
elaborate urns ornament each end of the terrace.

34

*The Museum Guest House for the guests of the Museum of Modern Art, at 242 East Fifty-second Street. Designed in 1949 by Philip Johnson.*

The front consists of a first-story wall of glazed orange-brown brick surmounted by three picture windows having curtains that are always drawn.

*New York Stock Exchange at 10 Broad Street. Designed in 1900 by George B. Post. Sculpture in the pediment by J. Q. A. Ward and Paul W. Bartlett. (J. B. Bayley)*

The high base here carries a giant Corinthian order. The base consists of two low stories, the upper one having balconied windows with voluted keystones. The giant order is framed at the sides by pilasters. It has an entablature and pediment with giant figures, while above there is a balustraded attic. The whole is actually "a false front" in the traditional American manner, for behind the columns is a glass wall enclosing one side of the large trading room of the Exchange.

*Principal front (facing north) of the General Assembly Building of the United Nations. Designed and built between 1947 and 1953 by an international board of architects, Wallace K. Harrison, chairman. (J. B. Bayley)*

The front consists of vertical strips of translucent marbled glass and marble. There is no ornament of any kind.

*Bronze flagpole base on the terrace of the New York Public Library at the corner of Forty-second Street and Fifth Avenue. Designed in 1912 by Thomas Hastings, executed by Raffaele J. Menconi and cast in the Tiffany Studios.*

Set on steps of stone, the base rests on turtles and a cable molding. Masks, garlands, cornucopias, and four winged figures ornament the lower portion. Egg-and-dart molding, voluted acanthus leaves, and small Zodiac signs are found on the next. At the third level bucranes (ox skulls), a favorite of ancient Rome, carry fluttering ribbons and garlands of fruit. Crowning the whole is a series of moldings, imbricated leaves and ornamented gadroons from which the flagpole rises.

*Bottom of the bronze flagpole on the terrace of the Seagram Building at Fifty-second Street and Park Avenue. Designed in 1955 and completed in 1958 by Ludwig Mies van der Rohe with Philip C. Johnson, associate.*

Mr. Mies van der Rohe has as motto the legend "Less Is More."

*The building of Duveen Brothers, 720 Fifth Avenue, which formerly stood on the northwest corner of Fifth Avenue and Fifty-sixth Street. Designed in 1911 by the architect René Sergent and associate, Horace Trumbauer. Destroyed in 1953. (Courtesy Duveen Brothers, Inc.)*

A rusticated base carries a giant Corinthian order which in turn supports an entablature, above which is a pediment with symbolic figures. An attic, skillfully placed behind the pediment, rises in a mansard. The ornamental details are many and varied. The voussoirs of the round arches of the ground-story are alternatively recessed to give the impression of strength. A central balcony with a balustrade is carried by two brackets in the shape of elaborate volutes from which hang swags of fruit.

*The Sabena Building, 720 Fifth Avenue, on the northwest corner of Fifth Avenue and Fifty-sixth Street. Designed in 1953 by Emery Roth & Sons. (J. B. Bayley)*

The above structure took the place of the Duveen Brothers building. Horizontal lines of glass alternate with horizontal lines of stone.

*Entrance to the apartment house at 131–135 East Sixty-sixth Street. Designed in 1905 by Charles Adams Platt.*

Immediately about the entrance is a frame of elaborate moldings, one with crossettes. Over the lintel is a large volute adorned with an acanthus leaf, presumably part of the support of the pediment. Actually the broken pediment rests on a broken entablature in turn supported by a pair of Ionic columns. Behind the columns the order is reflected in semi-pilasters.

*Entrance to the apartment house at 1025 Fifth Avenue. Designed in 1955 by Harold I. Feldman.*

No comment.

*Great Hall of the Cunard Building at 25 Broadway. Designed in 1921 by Benjamin Wistar Morris with Thomas Hastings, consultant. Stucco and fresco work by Ezra Winter. Maps by Barry Faulkner. Ironwork by Samuel Yellin. Bronze floor seal by John Gregory. (W. A. Probst, courtesy the Cunard Line)*

The hall consists of two square spaces with a large octagon in the middle; behind the splayed walls are domed alcoves, each twenty-two feet square, called luminary squares, since each opens to the outside and transmits daylight into the hall. The north and south sides of the two square spaces are extended by means of elliptical arches and roofed by groined arch ceilings, while the octagon in the middle has a dome sixty-five feet high. The walls and floor are of travertine. From a cornice thirty-five feet above the floor the ceiling springs with elaborate decoration in *fresco a secco* by Ezra Winter. The decoration is in a variety of classical detail mainly in cream, red, and blue, while placed in the ceiling at regular intervals are murals, with nudes and marine symbols in relief framed by lozenges.

*Main lobby of the Secretariat Building at the United Nations Headquarters, designed and built between 1947 and 1952 by an international board of architects with Wallace K. Harrison, chairman. (Courtesy United Nations)*

No comment.

# CHAPTER TWO

# The Superstition of the Modern

T HE City of Contrasts offers a strange spectacle: What is called Modern shrinks before an exuberant tradition, for the most part classical. If we today are perplexed at the transformation brought about by current fashion, future genera-tions will be even more so. Already the unornamented buildings appear as products of a generation faded in its own time. Why do we have such a spectacle, we may well ask, why is such desolation reserved for our era? In a land of plenty, need for economy offers no explanation, nor have political forces tipped the scale. The age does smile on us, but we in our architecture, and in all the arts, for that matter, are unable to smile back. The answer seems to lie in the current fashion and the forces behind it.

Fashion in architecture is neither capricious nor trivial; there are reasons for the Modern as there are reasons for its approaching demise. Fashion may be defined as the ruling convention in costume, in the arts, and in human interests generally; in architecture today's convention is the barren. How it came about is not hard to discover; the fashion sprang from a craving for originality. To be original, to be absolutely new, is not a case of differing from one's contemporaries —most Modern buildings look alike—but of being completely free of the past or "to be of our time," as the phrase goes. We must proclaim our era. Those con-sidered the most original are paradoxically the most honored in the imitation. The consequence is that originality has taken the place of beauty, the traditional aim of the architect.

The emphasis springs in part from today's conception of the individual who is constantly bidden to "express himself," presumably to announce individuality; our age must "express itself" by being consciously different. A misinterpretation of history has prodded the urge. History has been conveniently boxed into different epochs, each with heroes, qualities, and products, for an easier understanding of it, and especially has art history been neatly ticketed and placed in pigeonholes. What was at first a useful method of cataloguing and of furnishing insight is now seen as a series of art forms or "expressions" over the centuries, important because they are different or original. If past epochs have "expressed" themselves, we too must indulge the urge, and to be of our time we must be different regardless of cost in terms of beauty. The craving is seen in such phrases as "a valid search for form," "significant form," "creative expression," and "the struggle for new form." That we will be different whether we advance or do not advance under the ghostly banners of originality seems not to have been considered. Every age is by nature different; only a naïve age ignorant of lasting values would consciously make originality its only aim.

A certain rebelliousness has entered our attempts at self-assertion. Like spoiled children we must announce our presence loudly. Approximately thirty years ago, when the Modern was not quite as old as it is today, the designer who offered his stripped building enjoyed the astonishment, anger, and confusion that resulted. To shock came to be the mark of a new generation which was tossing aside the ideas and customs of its elders. An outspoken freedom in manners and morals was the rule of the day, and to be Modern in the arts—it was also true of poetry and prose—was reflection of the new-found freedom. Fixed in our rebel's mind was the illusion that Modern architecture would change the world, and some declared that the "revolution" in architecture would forestall political revolution, which had been so much a part of World War I. The reform aspect of the Modern is still very much with us, although its use as a counterweight to political revolution is not altogether clear.

In the nineteenth century originality had been attempted by combining ornament of different kinds, by turning to obscure styles such as the Romanesque, by strange asymmetry. The results, to be found in our older communities, draw gentle mockery from most, although Modern art historians judge the products in all seriousness. Such efforts would not do for our era; the Modernist had to have originality in the fullest sense of the term and he found the solution in contemporary painting. Painters, touched by the same urgency, came on the abstract soon after the turn of the century, and by its very definition the abstract offered a key. It is a way of making non-imitative patterns out of a void; there was no need to look at the past at all. It fitted neatly into architecture, where abstract forms are implicit, being one of the elements of design, although until now never the only element.

If originality spurred on the yearning for the abstract, it was reinforced by the division among the arts. Each one began striving in the course of the last century to take the lone road until, in our time, each has achieved autonomy. Painting and sculpture are no longer a part of architecture. As the divorce proceeded each art stripped itself of all subject matter and symbolism, among other elements. The artist became a hermit in the desert of his art with himself as god and found sterility under the label of purity. The emasculation in poetry reached the point a generation ago where language was reduced to mumbling and the results were laughed out of existence, but in the visual arts our abstractionists are still obsessed by the desert and sterility.

The abstract offered an additional charm. It was divorced not only from the past but from the outer world, the world of people, objects, images, and even ideas. Like the abstract painter who turns to his inner world to discover the voice

of genius, the architect can do the same and offer what he heard in terms of concrete, steel, and glass; by inference this inner world of primal forces, completely
cut off from the outside, is purer and finer. The artist who was once objective has
now become subjective, intent only on finding interior phantasms. The architect's
drive to break away from life has confirmed the divorce from the past and, in the
process of restricting his contemplation to himself, he has taken on a highly
mystical air. Although the mystical aspect of Modern buildings has often escaped
the beholder, he will find evidence of it in the writings of more than one architect
trying to explain his abstraction.

Joined to the mystical is the unlikely element of progress, transforming the
Modern from an experiment of the few into a fashion for the many. Progress in
its generally accepted sense was one of the important concepts of the last century,
reflected in the advance of the natural sciences and of material well-being, and
today it is a notion well nigh universal in its acceptance. Inevitably it has colored
all aspects of life, including the arts. Technical improvements in construction, new
techniques of painting, and new methods of making sculpture are declared to be
art forms; the notion is applied to art history, which is looked on as a progression
of original creations, although where the progress lies, let us say from Michelangelo
to Frank Lloyd Wright, is difficult to see. With the emergence of the abstract we
had presumably entered another phase of progress, and to be rid of ornament, in
itself supremely objective, was a sign that we were going forward.

Somehow to all the straining for the new there is a familiar ring. We have
heard before now diatribes against the menace of the past and the need for
progress in the arts; it was not very long ago and the complaining voices were
American. In the 1830's and 1840's many of our writers condemned the past
directly, and indirectly by denouncing Europe; they proclaimed a crusade for
American literature, forgetting that all that is written by an American or in
America is American. James Russell Lowell was among the crowd when he asked
our forebears in bad verse to

> Forget Europe wholly, your veins throb with blood,
> To which the dull current in hers is but mud.

Lowell grew out of the youthful fear and became our minister to the Court of St.
James. Horatio Greenough, who spent pleasant years studying sculpture under a
Florentine sky, told Emerson that "he would stop commerce, if he could, would
insulate the American to stop the foreign influence that denationalizes him."
Emerson himself fell into the error, having this message for artists that "nature
being the same on the banks of the Kennebec as on the banks of the Tiber—why
go to Europe?" William Morris Hunt and Elihu Vedder refused to let this pass
unchallenged and they called on the Sage of Concord. "Take from your shelves
your Bible, Plato, Shakespeare, Dante, Bacon, Montaigne, etc. and make it that
you could not consult them without going to Europe . . ." said the two painters.
"Yes, yes," was Emerson's vapid reply, "that is certainly an aspect of the question
which should be taken into consideration."

The fear of the past and of the influence of art with which Europe was so closely identified was satirized at the time. "We do not want art and refinement. We want genius—untutored, wild, original, free," exclaims a character in a Long-fellow novel; the author offers a succinct picture of some of today's architects. Hawthorne was very conscious of the nonsense and mocked it in "Earth's Holocaust," a tale to be found in *Mosses from an Old Manse*. With sudden inspiration man built himself a huge bonfire on the Western prairie (a site selected on the advice of a cautious insurance man), so runs the story, where inherited "outworn trumpery" was offered to the flames. The trumpery symbolized inherited evil. "Now we shall get rid of the weight of dead men's thoughts," cried the destroyers. When everything had been destroyed—and that included objects of art and books as well as ceremonial robes—they discovered that the evil of which they had hoped to rid the world was still there—in their own hearts.

Hawthorne also pictured the rebel against the past in the familiar *House of the Seven Gables*. The reader will recall Holgrave, the young daguerreotypist, who fell in love with Phoebe Pyncheon. "Shall we never, never get rid of this Past? It lies upon the present like a giant's dead body!" exclaimed the artist to the patient Phoebe. "But we shall live to see the day, I trust," he went on, "when no man shall build his house for posterity. Why should he? . . . If each generation were allowed and expected to build its own houses, that single change, comparatively unimportant in itself, would imply almost every reform which society is now suffering for. I doubt whether even our public edifices—our capitols, state-houses, court-houses, city halls, and churches—ought to be built of such permanent materials as stone or brick. It were better that they should crumble to ruin in twenty years, or thereabouts, as a hint to the people to examine into and reform the institutions which they symbolize." Hawthorne's irony has divined the present only too well. We have achieved Holgrave's buildings of impermanence, buildings which, although they will not crumble, will always hold the threat of doing so.

Originality, the abstract, false progress, fear of the past, and the sense of impermanence have become one, packaged in a wrapping called Modern. Although contemporary work of any period has been known in its own time as Modern, only today has the term won a capital and its present identification. Few words have known such respectability and promise: so rich in meaning is it that it describes and judges at the same time. It has even pre-empted the right to call architecture without ornament the only valid work of our time, a judgment which is history's privilege after all.

The wrapping called Modern only confirms the reaction against the styles of the past. In fact it professes not to be a style at all, let alone a fashion. It aspires to perpetuity. What is obviously temporary is made to appear inviolate by means of the label, an unconscious attempt to make fashion immovable and to transform it into taste, a very different article. Today's rebels are under the illusion that they can preserve their hegemony thanks to a name.

At this point it would be well to clear up the distinction, so often lacking, between fashion and taste. When most people speak of taste, they mean fashion; books purporting to be on taste are, with rare exception, such as Geoffrey Scott's

*The Great Hall of New York's Pennsylvania Station, designed in 1906 by Charles Follen McKim, of McKim, Mead & White. One of the great monumental interiors in American architecture has been subjected to contemporary visual destruction. The devices and materials of today offer an obvious sense of impermanence in contrast to the permanent sensation of the classical hall.*

*The Architecture of Humanism,* about fashion. As we have seen, fashion is a prevalent convention in the arts or dress; taste, on the other hand, is knowledge and perception of the best examples of man's work, the most beautiful or whatever is superior, especially in the fine arts. Taste resides in the permanent, fashion in the impermanent; taste has standards, fashion conventions.

At one time taste in the fine arts was acquired by the study of the best that man had created in the past. It called for severe discipline, systematic exercises for the eye, command of the art in the fullest sense, and self-control, which brings the only freedom. In architecture it meant knowledge, not only of buildings of all

50

kinds, but of decoration of all kinds, of the sister arts from painting to cabinet-making. The professional parted from the connoisseur in knowing construction techniques and how to draw well. A complete mastery of the Five Orders (Doric, Ionic, Corinthian, Composite, and Tuscan) and the ability to draw the human figure were considered essential. Nor was a broad culture to be despised, because the past in all its facets can shape taste. Placing so much emphasis on the absolutely new, the Modernists have disowned traditional taste. Instead they offer another, a form of conscious, and at times unconscious, reasoning limited to the function and construction of a building. On one level the reasoning leads to an architecture where the specified functions are met, as nearly as possible, by absolute efficiency and economy, and on the other by an architecture which announces its *function* by a game of structural logic, presenting a visual argument of its methods. The first is based on the narrow premises of a mathematical architecture, a slide-rule solution. Although frequently attempted it never proceeds beyond the experimental stage; it is a form of engineering rather than architecture. The second approach allows a variety of structural experimentation as long as the *function* of the building is accepted as of sufficient impact to make its presence interesting. "Form follows function" is the rebel's slogan as he wheels out his makeshift formula.

Today's synthetic taste in architecture is restricted to knowing how to meet certain limited necessities by playing with construction, plan, and materials where the play is revealed to the beholder. The result, a form of structural dialectics, is called "functional." The theory can be applied to all kinds of buildings and artifacts, with the consequence that everything is leveled. An Indian tepee, a Japanese peasant hut, or the latest Modern building takes on the same value as the Lincoln Memorial. Styles of the past are judged according to "efficiency" or how they fit into the pattern of the current functional. A formula has been arrived at which requires no knowledge of the past because it is enough to grasp structural dialectics to judge a building or achieve original architecture.

The rules of the game call for strict obedience to the exigencies of construction, plan, and materials, each one fixed in a special context. Construction must be revealed, the plan must determine the elevation or be "expressed" on the exterior, and the materials can be employed only "in their nature." If some insist on using ornament, it must be timidly present and have no reference to the past; instead of ornament, greenery in the form of bushes, vines, and trees is permitted. It is a game which is played under the closest supervision of editors of art and architectural magazines, museum officials, art critics, professors of architecture, and successful Modern architects. One tragic consequence has been that the Modern has become America's official architecture abroad; each new consulate, embassy, or chancellory combines originality, the abstract and false progress and reflects the fear of the past and the sense of impermanence.

The trinity of construction, plan and materials in the Modern orthodoxy is to be found conjointly in most recent buildings. In the smaller ones and in the simpler artifacts we sometimes find one or two of the three isolated. It is one of

51

*Interior of the New Wing (1953) of the Yale University Art Gallery and Design Center by Louis I. Kahn. A good example of a reinforced concrete interior where the concrete has been left exactly as it came from the wooden forms. The tetrahedrons which form the ceiling are actually a modified system of concrete T-beams with deep inclined stems combined with triangular inclined bridging elements. The architect, who believes that the ornament of our age will stem from methods of construction, "loves the construction joint, the form imprint . . ." (Lionel Freedman)*

the assumptions of today that the most functional or efficient can be called "good design," that is when the designer restricts himself to the mechanical aspect of his work. A typical product is the new lamppost now found on New York streets where a pole of stainless steel rises, unadorned and inviolate, to an unadorned head. In the New York Port Authority Bus Terminal the designers have produced an original building by letting the construction and plan dictate the exterior. The curved front "expresses" the curve of the interior ramp required by the busses. The new wing of the Yale University Art Gallery is a sample of rigid control of the trinity. On the interior, instead of covering the walls, ceilings, and piers with a revetment of marble, plaster, or wood, the reinforced concrete frame of the structure has been left exactly as it came from the wooden forms. The texture of the concrete is considered of sufficient value to interest the beholder; as can be imagined it forms a somewhat sombre background to many of the objects on display. The pattern of the ceiling takes its shape from a system of construction called tetrahedral space slab, left exposed to permit us to admire the structural dialectic. Outside, facing the street, rises a sixty-foot blank wall, an expression of brick, and horizontal strips of stone denote the floor levels.

Accent on the plan is often made in the name of the trinity, particularly in country and suburban houses. The kitchen, dining room, and living room are made one and given an irregular plan called "free-flowing." Useful rooms such as the vestibule and library are rejected; they have been joined to the "living area." A lack of privacy is one of the conditions of the Modern house; every inch of space must be pre-empted, an aim often achieved at considerable additional cost; the functional look must be there. All of this applies with equal validity to the Modern church, where some extraordinary shapes have been achieved thanks to structural caprice.

An emphasis on materials, the last of the trinity, can carry novelty to a high degree. The Fifth Avenue branch of the Manufacturers Trust Company shows how glass alone can be made into a plain abstract pattern; the material, as it is said, is being expressed. A similar effect is to be found in Lever House on Park Avenue. The arch for the Jefferson Memorial Park expresses stainless steel and, of course, forbids the use of sculpture. Reinforced concrete, the cinder block, stainless steel, aluminum, and, above all, glass are considered pre-eminently Modern. Yet Edward D. Stone, the much-acclaimed architect of the United States Pavilion at the Brussels Exposition who, as one of the designers of the Museum of Modern Art, was among these responsible for introducing walls of glass, has this to say about the functional aspect of the material: "Let's face it. Large glass areas create serious problems. Interiors are hard to heat in winter and to cool in summer. The problem of glare is continuous." He himself has now turned to the cement grille following the lead of the late French Modernist, Auguste Perret. Yet glass remains in vogue because it makes a heavy demand on structural techniques which, perforce, must be revealed, it eliminates ordinary walls, thus taking away the opportunity to adorn, and presumably it joins the indoors and outdoors, a step which is claimed to be "natural."

The formula has been accompanied by a vocabulary of its own, for the one of traditional taste had to be rejected. Such words as "honest" and "false," at one time reserved for describing the human character, have come to be current in architecture. A building is "honest" when the structure is revealed, "false" when concealed. Moral standards have come to be applied to buildings as if a construction method or building material can be defined in moral terms. "Pure" was an early favorite to describe something devoid of ornament, and the Franco-Swiss Modernist, Le Corbusier, has gone to the length of inventing an abstract movement called "purism." "Clean," another synonym for functional, is also in favor as seen in "clean lines," clean surfaces" meaning that there is no ornament, while "clean engineering" means visible structure. As if these were not enough, a number of others, once reserved for the natural sciences have been taken over, such as "organic," "natural," and "crystalline," and from philosophy has come "pragmatic." A low one-story house, formerly called a bungalow, is an "organic structure" because it spreads over the ground; earth-clinging, it is "natural" where a two-story house is not. Mysticism has touched such terms as "hygienic" and "antiseptic," both words of praise, all of them implying a certain moral superiority of the Modern over the classical manner of building. Our latter-day iconoclast is puritanical in his outlook on the arts in a way which would astonish our Puritan ancestors. Besides conveying the false moral note the mystical words proclaim the break with the past, a "Revolution of the Word," to sanctify the rebellion. (A change is currently taking place in some Modernist circles. The once hated word "beauty" is coming back, but "pure" has not been dropped altogether, for when they mention beauty it is "pure beauty.")

Mixed with the false moral note is a pseudoscientific approach reflected in the mechanical justification of design. The achievements of the natural sciences are wonderful and the scientific method is often of value, but a blind application of either to the arts can be disastrous. This is especially so when the artist makes use of scientific facts which the scientist himself has long discarded. "Facts change color, meaning, and substance in accordance with the sovereign concept that marshalls them," Arthur Upham Pope has written; the authority on Persia was asking for caution in the use of scientific method in cultural activities. With the Modernist it is enough that everything looks "scientific" or is described in scientific terms to assure the world that he is as scientific as he is moral when it comes to building. The anxiety to achieve the "scientific look" at all cost explains why so many Modern buildings and pieces of furniture are expensive and non-functional.

Already the fashion that would be taste has its academy, far more rigid and orthodox than the old classical academy. Without a single exception education in the nation's architectural schools is confined to the "form follows function" approach. Textbooks have been written according to Modern strictures, and lately an emasculated form of history has been admitted to provide a prop for today's originality. Yet with all their orthodoxy and power, ensconced as they are in key positions in museums, architectural firms, and schools, the Modernists remain uneasy. They who once prided themselves on being rebels are no longer rebellious. Against whom can the heroes of this "permanent revolution" raise their swords? All is not comfort in the bare office whose very aspect is a sign of weakness. Their contempt for the past and the living world about them, as a former trustee of the American Academy in Rome remarked to the author, is the best evidence by far that we are witnessing a temporary craze. No doubt there will be plenty of high blood pressure when the inevitable change takes place, but it will not stop the coming of a new architecture, new painting, and new sculpture when taste in its traditional sense, i.e., knowledge of the best examples of classical art, once again takes command.

With the approaching demise of the so-called Modern it is not without value to consider another name for its efforts. The term "Modern" is hardly satisfactory as a label for the ultimate convulsive phase of an aging movement. In its place we offer the label "Picturesque Secessionism" because it explains and defines. We have seen that functional architecture is an attempted rebellion or secession from historical styles with emphasis on the mechanics of construction and that its dominating goal is to be original, that is, strange, unusual, and accidental but not beautiful or sublime, in a word, "picturesque." Modern being a term applied to any contemporary work in any period, the title of Picturesque Secessionism is far more satisfactory.

If evidence is still wanting on the bankruptcy of Secessionism, it can be observed that an architectural style which boasts of no higher aim than the functional restricts itself to the meanest solutions. Any work where something more than the material end is called for, namely monumental buildings, lies beyond its reach. The Bus Terminal of the New York Port Authority is such a building. There is no question of its capacity to take care of busses and passengers, its roof is an admirable parking space, and its façade is shaped by the plan, but it is an ugly building. Here is one of the important buildings of a large city, a daily gateway for thousands, and there is a total lack of inspiration. (The airline terminals in the city are equally indifferent.)

By contrast the Grand Central Terminal is magnificent, bidding a superb welcome to all who go to and from the city. To achieve his end, Whitney Warren designed a façade that, besides the giant bays and paired columns, has the crowning feature of a colossal Mercury who motions to us to view the splendor that transportation has created. Warren knew that he would not achieve the desired sense of inspiration without sculpture or painting, not as an afterthought but as an essential part of the fabric. To this end he persuaded William Kissam Vanderbilt, who controlled the New York Central Railroad, to allow Jules-Alexis Coutan to do the sculptured group. The artist recognized the challenge, defining his end thus: "To give the vitality of the present to a symbolism that is consecrated by centuries of literature and art and philosophy." With Warren's blessing Paul Helleu produced the famous starry ceiling of the great hall; a latter-day Joshua, the French painter bade the heavens be still to invite our wonder. No Picturesque Secessionist terminal can even attempt to rival the Grand Central or any other of our great classical terminals, because today's designer refuses to recognize the theatrical, nay operatic, qualities of art. Should he invite his colleagues in sculpture and painting to help him, the result is meaningless abstract work, and at that the invitation is extended shabbily. At most he can place the work, as the De Rivera sculpture at 711 Third Avenue, to one side like a hotel sticker on a piece of baggage, without the welcome of a setting or frame. As for making

*The best piece of monumental sculpture in America, the Mercury group on the attic of Grand Central Terminal in New York, Jules-Alexis Coutan sculptor. Hercules, or Physical Energy, is the figure on the left, that on the right is Minerva, or Moral Energy. A giant eagle with spreading wings the national symbol, stands behind Mercury. The figure of Mercury is twenty-eight feet high, his arm nine feet long. The golden lantern of the New York Central Building is in the background.*

use of the human form, like Elie Nadelman's water god at 40 Wall Street, he is far too frightened of it to try. "Painting and sculpture are abandoned," the French poet Paul Valéry lamented twenty years ago. "Their mother architecture is dead. As long as she lived she offered them a place, an occupation and qualifications. Freedom to wander was refused them. They had their space, their well-defined light, their subject matter and their federations . . ."

The illusion of equating the functional with the beautiful could not be better illustrated than in New York's latest lamppost, a mediocre adornment for a great city. The old one, with its plentiful detail and its pleasing shape, is a handsome ornament. What is more, it is a symbol for the city, and its passing occasions sorrow, a reward the new one will never know.

Typical of so much of Modern striving is the Kaufmann house by Frank Lloyd Wright. Technical proficiency, emphasis on texture, the "open" plan, and the yoking with nature (it is built over a waterfall) add up to no more than an eccentricity. It is a relief to turn to the Diego Suarez villa, by Frederic Rhinelander King, which reflects architecture in the true sense of the term. The building has

56

sculpture and ornamental detail, it has a formal plan, it makes use of nature as a setting, not as a shroud. No doubt some will point an accusing finger at the villa's formal garden and speak of nature contravened, emphasizing the cost of maintenance. The lover of nature and economy may be upset to learn that, behind the waterfall over which it is built, the Kaufmann house boasts of a "natural" pool heated to bathtub temperature. Wright is an architect who bars sculpture on the exterior and leaves no place on the interior for pictures, because of the low ceilings and irregular walls. King, on the other hand, makes place for sculpture and other ornament, offers high ceilings and walls to welcome pictures. The one by denying the past has found an originality which will die with him; the other by steeping himself in the past has found the beauty which beckons to the future.

We move from one aberration to another, from the Socony Mobil Building to the Fifth Avenue branch of the Manufacturers Trust Company. Mechanical skill, use of stainless steel, quantities of glass, air-conditioning equipment, high-speed elevators, escalators, and other technical triumphs make for nothing but greater ugliness which has been praised by the Modernists as "The New Brutality." The shock element has paid off well in many instances, but where will be the shock when all the streets are of steel and glass? Must we wait for a new structural device or a new material to shock another decade? "All the metal and glass that ever were melted," wrote Ruskin, "have not so much weight in them as will clog the wings of one human spirit's aspiration."

We might examine the City of Contrasts in every detail, yet each time the architecture of the styles would outweigh the Modern. In the one the artist accepted the challenge of his art, in the other he avoids it by declaring his aim to be functional and prefers the name of engineer to artist. Should the functional not offer the death's-head grin of a structural skeleton, it is distorted by the attempt at originality. Years ago men knew that to run after originality would lead to the quaint and the monstrous, and such is today's reward, held as we are by the superstition of the Modern.

Visual destruction is everywhere about us. Just as many painters take the nude apart and offer pieces of it in a syllabus of destruction like a Picasso painting, the Secessionist architect creates disorder by his design. The aesthetic vivisection still to be found on canvas is also on the drafting board. Instead of placing columns on a building, the building is placed on stilts, as in Lever House. The cottage by the waterfall has been replaced by the elephantine bungalow on top of the waterfall, vide the Kaufmann residence. The Museum Guest House on Fifty-second Street in New York has turned its back to the passer-by, destroying the ordinary conception that man should offer a pleasing façade to the world. The lobby of the General Assembly Building of the United Nations is a structural vivisection out of a German movie of the 1920's. The Shed at Lenox is a negation of art, but at least it has been well named.

A seeming paradox lies in the struggle for originality. Why, if the aim is so important today, do so many Modern buildings look alike? One explanation is simple enough: By denying the past the Secessionist gives undue importance to his contemporaries; knowing only their work, he can do no more than imitate them. (The building on stilts, as in the example of Lever House, was taken directly from Le Corbusier.) A second reason lies in the limitation of the functional theory. With all ornament ruled out architecture has banished freedom. Like a musician satisfied with one note to his piccolo, the Modernist has already exhausted his few themes, and no new techniques or materials can vary the tune. "His work," wrote the novelist François Mauriac recently of a very successful original painter, "extends like a dead sea over a dead world, spiritually dead."

The saddest consequence of originality is the element of destruction. Visual disorder, too much with us under any circumstance, has been compounded. Chaos reigns supreme as the drive to be original destroys the harmony we have inherited, not only in individual buildings but also in the urban scene and in the landscape. Today, not content with excluding the past, we must strike out at the work of our predecessors and try to crush it. "In order to get organic architecture born," Frank Lloyd Wright, architect of the Solomon R. Guggenheim Museum, has told us, "intelligent architects will be forced to turn their backs on antique rubbish heaps with which classic eclecticism has encumbered our new ground."

*Main public entrance of the General Assembly Building of the United Nations, designed and built between 1947 and 1953 under an international board of architects, Wallace K. Harrison chairman. The ramp and the balconies offer a good example of structural dialectics, in this instance playing with the cantilever. The Modernist delight in exposing structure and machinery is shown by open beams and ducts in the ceiling. (Courtesy United Nations)*

*Schlosstheater in the Schönbrunn Palace, Vienna, designed in 1766–67 by Johann Ferdinand von Hohenberg. (Courtesy Austrian Information Service.) Music by Mozart, once played in the theater, is today played in the "Shed" (below), the Summer Opera House, Berkshire Music Center at Tanglewood near Lenox, Mass. Designed in 1940 by Eliel and Eero Saarinen. (Will Plouffe Studio, courtesy Boston Symphony Orchestra)*

We may presume that he means, among others, the National Capitol. And Hilla Rebay, former director of the same museum, went him one better. "It is really a pity," she wrote in 1950 to a European correspondent, "that the bombs [of the last war] did not do their job more thoroughly in wiping out the old." Plutarch recorded that one Eratostratus set fire to the famous Temple of Diana of Ephesus on the night that Alexander the Great was born. When asked the reason for his action he confessed that he desired to make his name eternal. Perhaps the Secessionists, like Eratostratus, will one day know immortality for having attempted to destroy the temple of our classical heritage.

Not without reason do they want to destroy the past; it has such a persistent way of mocking their puny efforts. The old wing of the Yale University Art Gallery has ornament, scale, and proportion, all things absent in the new wing. One of the unforeseen consequences of the destruction has been the rapidly growing appreciation of our ornamental past and of the art that created it, an indication that the public is growing impatient with the spreading ugliness and brutality.

Yet we are told that the disorder of Picturesque Secessionism is nothing more or less than an order we do not perceive. This is sophistry, an attempt to confuse; the functional theory and the aim of originality are nothing less than nihilism, a nihilism radiating a curious *mystique*. At best it is indifference to humanity, at worst perversity to the point of being evil. It is hardly surprising that the fashion will never become taste.

If we once accept the consequence of present fashion as a form of nihilism, then the Modern can no longer be termed "progress." In truth, it is retrogressive because it denies ornament, an essential product of man's instinct, in part a product of his own reason visually embodied. Man must fill a void, make his mark, draw a line across the canvas. It is backward to be at the mercy of techniques and materials; the truly progressive architect bids the engineer work for him and he makes use of engineering devices, not for their own sake, nor as abstractions, but to build a beautiful building. To bar curiosity by erasing the past is to tie one's hands in approaching the future. Man is made up of the community of the past, the present, and the future, and he must have all three to go forward. Further, it is retrogressive to invite disorder. In architecture order and harmony are of the essence; to deny them is to deny beauty, and to deny beauty, a part of life, is to deny true progress. In an ever-changing world man needs the permanence of beauty, that quasi-sacred beauty which only the arts can bring. Hawthorne knew this. Toward the close of *The House of the Seven Gables,* he has the rebellious Holgrave coming to admire stone architecture because "the exterior, through the lapse of years, might have been adding venerableness to its original beauty, and thus giving that impression of permanence which I consider essential to the happiness of any one moment." It is the tragedy of our time that glass, steel, and other much-touted materials will never achieve the patina, texture, and complexion which conveys the passage of time and the sense of permanence.

With the approaching demise of Picturesque Secessionism, it is obvious that we must begin all over again. Taste must be rediscovered and renewed. We must learn its standards, know how to make use of them, and respect the monuments it calls great. We must admit that the word "functional," to have value, must be blessed with a meaning over and above the mechanical, that it includes ornament to please the eye, and that it welcomes the past because man loves grandeur which has meaning in terms of his heritage.

It is then, and only then, that we will have a fashion which has strong roots in our past, a fashion which will be bound by ancient tradition. There is such a quality as American taste, and we will find it by looking to the best of our inheritance. The key to the future lies there. An artistic fashion of abundance and happiness, not of meanness and denial, will be our reward.

its standards, know how to make use of them, and respect the monuments it calls great. We must admit that the word "functional," to have value, must be blessed with a meaning over and above the mechanical, that it includes ornament to please the eye, and that it welcomes the past because man loves grandeur which has meaning in terms of his heritage.

# CHAPTER THREE
# The American Contribution

OUR heritage? All things to all men, it is said, and yet it is not a kaleidoscope, ever revolving on the demand of fashion, offering elusive shapes and colors. Inevitably out of the past some generations stand in bold relief, some works claim precedence, some heroes cast their shadows on the present, and some jewels of art shine brighter than others. Before the mass offering of our heritage we are bound to select and distinguish. What has pleased man once and pleased him again will surely please us, for time alone is privileged to single out the best. And in knowing and perceiving the best we will achieve taste.

The Secessionist, who cannot escape history altogether, would have us select as inspiration the inventions in the construction industry and the examples of self-conscious originality, along with a smattering of folk art. The balloon frame, the cast-iron front, and the steel frame are termed peculiarly American and therefore worthy of study. So too are original buildings, be they the megalithic work of Henry Hobson Richardson, or an *art nouveau* product of Louis Sullivan, or a "prairie style" suburban villa by Frank Lloyd Wright. The balloon frame was an advance in wood construction which permitted the rise overnight of cities like San Francisco and Chicago in the 1850's, but the result was hardly art. The steel frame made possible the tall building, but again it does not follow that it produced beauty. To write of our architecture in that way is like telling the history of Venetian architecture in terms of pile-driving or that of the English in the evolving use of iron tie-rods. Buildings which have only originality to boast of, such as the work of Louis Sullivan, remain curiosities, not inspirations. Sullivan's ornament was so original that it died with him, and that too will be the fate of Wright's special manner. For many technique and originality are too plain an historical diet, and so folk art is accepted as adequate sauce. Primitive houses and farms with their homemade furniture and objects are singled out for being especially American, yet it is too often overlooked that their attraction is not so much the simplicity as the classical detail often present. Structural innovations and attempts at originality are of consequence to the scientific and social historian; most folk art belongs in an anthropological museum or with an historical society, and only a few can be ranged with the fine arts.

There is a second approach, also Secessionist, which has an entirely personal basis. Buildings are singled out and explained by criteria belonging more properly to economic and social history rather than by aesthetic standards. Architecture is said to be a reflection of ambition, of wealth, of new money, of the income tax or what-have-you. All of these may help to explain trends in fashion or to account for a given building, but they in no way tell us why one building is superior to another. We are invited to look at the personality of the architect and asked to dwell on his struggles more than on his work. Architecture in this instance is a delightful Old Farmer's Almanack where we may pick and choose at our pleasure. Such a purely subjective approach is often very entertaining and rewarding, but it cannot lead us to a heritage that offers standards.

It is not unlike a third, more popular, way of looking at our architecture where the universal catalogue is substituted for the personal. Both paths lead to an acceptance of all eras and their works in the same light and with the same degree of attention as if each succeeding generation achieved equal stature. We have forgotten that "it is only an auctioneer who can equally and impartially admire all schools of art," as Oscar Wilde remarked. Such misguided efforts condemn us as a people to an amorphous and chaotic inheritance with no standards at all.

Taste in the fine arts, it must be admitted, lies in appreciating the best. Not everything will pass muster, only that which has had the approval of time. Perhaps Thomas Jefferson can lend a guiding hand here, for he, more than any other of our heroes, watched over the nation's taste. When it came to selecting a design for the Virginia Capitol, he wrote from Paris that "in the execution of those orders [for drawings] two methods of proceeding presented themselves to my mind. The one was to leave to some architect to draw an external according to his fancy, in which way experience shews that about once in a thousand times a pleasing form is hit upon; the other was to take some model already devised and approved by the general suffrage of the world. I had no hesitation in deciding that the latter was best, nor after the hesitation was there any doubt what model to take. There is at Nismes in the South of France a building, called the Maison quarrée, erected in the time of the Caesars . . . We know that [it] . . . has pleased universally for near 2000 years." Our architecture for him had to find inspiration in the famous building of the past. "Whenever it is proposed to prepare plans for the Capitol, I should prefer the adoption of some one of the models of antiquity, which have had the approbation of thousands of years . . ." was his message in 1791 to Major L'Enfant, then laying out the city of Washington. By "the models of antiquity" he meant particularly the Roman; our inspiration had to be "Roman taste, genius and magnificence," as he put it. If he believed that the road to taste was the classical one for the young republic, we would be foolish not to look at it in our own time. America's contribution to architecture does not lie in technical achievements, originality, folk art, or the fact that many of its large private houses were paid for by newly made fortunes; in truth, it lies in adapting the classical tradition and, to a much lesser degree, the Gothic to our needs and our desires. Viewing the panorama of our architectural heritage, we see at once the role of the classical:

63

The American baroque or Georgian of colonial times, the American Roman or federal of the young republic, the Greek revival of the romantic era, the Second Empire of the Civil War era, and the American Renaissance from 1880 to 1930. Until very recently the architecture of the federal government stood fast to the classical tradition. If historians have played down our classical heritage, owing to the vogue of the Modern, it still stands triumphantly about us. The examples of it that follow are many and varied. For those who persist in asking for originality, the examples offered are original, for the classical is at once retrospective and ever new. The backward glance transforms and regenerates. Every generation of classical architecture has its own vision of perfection and its own Golden City. The examples are American as is all that is built on American soil. Let us follow Jefferson's counsel and look to our classical best in our search for taste.

It means that we will have to go along the familiar highway of American history and look at the familiar with a fresh eye. There is reward in rediscovery which will help us on our way, and there are not a few surprises.

*A typical example of colonial invention, use of wood like stone, is found in the Went-worth-Gardiner House (1760) in Portsmouth, New Hampshire. Rustication, quoins, the door frame with its pediment, cornice and window trim are all part of the effort to offer the best possible front to the world. (Wayne Andrews)*

Inevitably local conditions of climate, building materials, and new skills forced the colonists in the seventeenth century to devise a new architecture. The half timber and thatch of the old country were soon forgotten in English America for the clapboard and shingle. The house that resulted was still a reminder of the medieval, with its overhanging second story and small windows, and it was also a very plain affair. When affluence began to smile on the struggling colonies, a new style appeared from England, that of Sir Christopher Wren and his followers, the men who made the English baroque. Up to this time the colonists had confined themselves to domestic architecture; with the coming of the baroque a church architecture appeared. Two main conditions forced them to reinterpret the style when it crossed the Atlantic. The first was the question of materials. What had been a stone and brick architecture in England became a wood and wood-and-brick architecture here. And, secondly, the American work was modest in size and extent. Neither conditions restrained the native designer or carpenter; the obstacles served only to encourage them to make the best of the materials at hand.

*Mount Vernon (1757–87), the home of George Washington, has many devices derided by Modernists. One of them is exterior woodwork which is rusticated, chamfered, and even sanded to give the impression of stone. (Courtesy Mount Vernon Ladies Association of the Union)*

The chief distinction was the adaption of classical ornament, both inside and outside, to woodwork. The clapboard house of New England, without ornament, was an original American structure and hardly one to be called distinguished. When it took on ornament, such as a swan's neck pediment, fluted pilasters, and a cornice, the house became elegant, something to boast about. The Wentworth-Gardiner house in Portsmouth, New Hampshire, is a good example of the quality attained by using classical detail. The builder in this instance carried decoration further than was customary by imitating stonework in the wooden walls. Giving the façade of a house so much detail made it more impressive, and in the same way the interior repeats the striving by making full use of ornament wherever possible. (Interestingly enough, there is a clapboard architecture in Norway, especially in Bergen. Lacking ornament of any kind, it does not invite our attention.)

Mount Vernon, George Washington's residence on the Potomac, is another example where exterior siding was rusticated and beveled to resemble blocks of masonry, as well as covered with a sanded paint to heighten the illusion. The first President carried this so-called falsification another step by having several false windows. The banquet room, which rises two stories, eliminates the second-story bedroom, making windows at the second story unnecessary. To have omitted them would have disturbed the symmetry of the façade; for that reason we find the two false ones. In the same spirit the colonist would paint his humble pine interior to resemble cedar (called "graining") or marble ("marbling") and, if it was his pleasure, *chinoiserie* might be found, as in the Vernon house in Newport.

The colonists were equally successful in adapting the style of the London churches built by Wren and others. One handsome London church, St. Martin's-in-the-Fields, by James Gibbs, has served as model for four American churches: The Center Church in New Haven (a post-Revolutionary sample of American baroque), St. Paul's Chapel in New York, Christ Church in Philadelphia, and St. Michael's in Charleston. All are handsome and all are different. The fact that we know the source of inspiration does not lessen the contribution they bring to the American scene; the city, in every instance, would be the poorer without them. The scholar can discover where this or that bit of ornament or plan had its origin, and their discoveries heighten our enjoyment of the building. Peter Harrison's Redwood Library in Newport is obviously modeled on a Palladian design, and he could not have chosen better.

It is a curious paradox that the log cabin, which we often consider peculiarly American because it is so closely identified with the early struggles in our past, is of Swedish or German origin. We evolved several forms of it, original specimens for those who must have originality. Yet all the originality in the world would not make the useful structure beautiful, and it is not surprising that it passed out of use as soon as our ancestors had the means of producing something better.

THE AMERICAN ROMAN

With the coming of independence the classical inspiration offered by the mother country proved inadequate. We have seen how Jefferson guided the nation

*An early example of the porticoed church, St. Michael's (1752–61) in Charleston. Prompted by London's St. Martin's-in-the-Fields, it has pilasters, keystones, engaged columns, rusticated voussoirs, and other artifices to engage the eye. The material is hard stucco on brick in imitation of stone. (Wayne Andrews)*

in the matter of taste; he had as his particular favorites the French classical, the ancient Roman, and his beloved Palladio. There was no longer any incentive to explore the past via the London gateway when all of Europe was open to Americans. We could now go to the sources in France and Italy as the English themselves had done for some time. By turning directly to the great classical examples we could attain, Jefferson believed, an architecture of pomp and glory worthy of a great republic. His Virginia Capitol at Richmond was one of the first, a Roman temple sheltering a seat of government. He adapted the Roman manner to a center of learning in his design for the University of Virginia; colonnades join the buildings, which face a green sward and lead to a library modeled on the Roman Pantheon.

In like fashion George Washington bent sympathetically over L'Enfant's plan for the Federal City. He approved of this vision, the product of classical France to be planted in American soil. The boulevards, allées, circles, and squares which had only known royal gardens and royal forests were introduced into a city as they never were before and too seldom since. While more challenging to the builder and the statesman the radio-concentric plan, for such it is, is more suitable than the familiar grid for placing buildings to advantage, for shaping vistas, and for contriving the settings of magnificence a great city must have.

Washington also found time to study the designs for the National Capitol. "The Dome which is suggested . . ." he wrote of one project, "would, in my opinion, give beauty and grandeur to the pile." In another he approved its suggestion of a grand colonnade. Of Dr. William Thornton's, the winning, design, he had nothing but praise. "The Grandeur, Simplicity and Beauty of the exterior; the propriety with which the apartments are distributed," he said in a letter in 1793, "and the economy in the mass of the whole structure will, I doubt not, give it preference in your eyes, as it has done in mine . . ." We can see the building we know so well being shaped in his mind. It was in this way that Americans took the dome, particularly the dome set on a drum, and placed it on a house of legislature to make it one of the symbols of the democratic state. Heretofore it had been, with rare exceptions, reserved for churches. Today, when we think of Washington, it is the dome of the Capitol which first comes to mind, and the fact that it has since been imitated in state capitols and some city halls serves only to confirm the symbolism.

The examples of beauty achieved in the years of the young republic are on every side. There is the White House of James Hoban, the Albany Academy by Philip Hooker, the Massachusetts State House with its gold dome by Charles Bulfinch and Mangin and McComb's New York City Hall, the jewel now surrounded by towers. Many of them have interiors (with objects of art) to match the exteriors in quality, especially the National Capitol. Benjamin Latrobe designed the chamber of the old House of Representatives, today Statuary Hall, and created a monumental décor in a small space with the blessing of beautiful stone. The room is semicircular in shape with a row of columns of mixed white, blue-gray, and black breccia on the round side, while above springs a coffered semidome with an oculus at the center. The flat wall opposite, with its ample frieze, once had an eagle on it, and below was a colossal figure of Liberty, while near the entrance were four relief figures, all by Giuseppe Franzoni, the first sculpture of its kind in a public building in the country. The statues were destroyed when the British burned the Capitol in 1814; what we see today is the restoration, also by Latrobe. For the full effect we must think of it when it was the House, with its benches, Speaker's dais, and red hangings; Samuel F. B. Morse has left a well-known picture of it, now in the

*The Rotunda of the National Capitol (1803–20), by Benjamin Latrobe and Charles Bulfinch, is America's supreme interior. On the walls are the famous historical canvases of John Trumbull commissioned by Congress in 1817.*

Corcoran Gallery. Despite later changes it remains one of the country's great rooms. The neighboring Rotunda, by Latrobe and his successor Bulfinch, is its monumental complement, its noble walls adorned by the historical canvases of John Trumbull, while overhead soars the great dome.

Even in the romantic era, dawn of a new fashion which was eventually to destroy the classical image, we find the classical persisting. The universal adoption of the temple form is one of the marks of the age of steamboats and sailing packets. Plantation houses in the South, country villas in the North, banks and government buildings everywhere were touched by the Greek revival. The Roman forms of the previous generation gave way to a very restrained classical which had a certain cold quality in the absence of sculptured detail.

Again the traveler will not find the equivalent easily outside the United States. Andalusia, the home of the famous opponent of Andrew Jackson, the banker Nicholas Biddle, sits calmly on a lawn overlooking the Delaware. Doric columns of wood ring the mansion. At the end of an alley of oaks on the lower Mississippi we can come on Greenwood, one of the great plantation dwellings in the Greek manner. Humbler residences up and down the Eastern seaboard and west to Texas have their columned porches and pilastered doorways. In town the banks of the era, identified by columns, catch the eye; the columned bank has continued to be, until very recently, a fixture of the American townscape. Churches, especially in small towns, maintained the tradition of the columned porch, and county courthouses, that peculiarly American feature, were seldom built without white columns.

The classical did not rule absolutely; inevitably the Neo-Gothic, which had become fashionable in Europe in the wake of Romantic poetry and novels, made its first appearance. Churches, naturally enough, were built in the style, largely on the model of medieval parish churches of England. Country mansions and villas reflected the penchant, and many remain to delight us, like the Harral-Wheeler house in Bridgeport, Connecticut. (As this book went to press, the Harral-Wheeler house was destroyed by the city of Bridgeport.) Yet the Gothic did not push aside the Greek, or for that matter the Tuscan, another classical style favored for houses.

Garden art was another story. The classical had prevailed up to the time of the Revolution, and in Jefferson's time, although he favored the English garden, the formal stayed on. With the Romantic era the classical was exiled from the landscape, largely as a result of the efforts of Andrew Jackson Downing. He planted the English manner so firmly it reached down to the smallest open lot. Not until the 1890's did the classical appear in the landscape again.

## THE CIVIL WAR ERA

About the mid-century America's industrial potential began to loom on the horizon. With the pace set by railroad construction, new techniques and materials were evolved and, as with wood a hundred years before, they served the classical.

In an era which lay so strongly under the influence of the French Second Empire the early French classical became the fashion. Its most conspicuous monuments are the old State, War-Navy Building in Washington and the city hall of Philadelphia; in both order is piled on order, ascending to a high mansard roof. Columns of cast iron, the new material of the day, are to be found in the former, as they are

*The interior of
the cathedral of
Saints Peter and Paul
in Philadelphia
(1846–64),
by Father Maller
and Tornatore and
the architect
Napoleon Le Brun.
An example of
the continuing classical
at the time of the
Civil War.
The apse was extended
in 1957.
(Don Pasquarella,
courtesy the*
Evening Bulletin,
*Philadelphia)*

*The New Orleans
Custom House,
designed by A. T. Wood
in 1849. A magnificent
marble interior reflects
the New Orleans of
the cotton-boom days.
(Richard Koch)*

in many large structures of the period; it was cast-iron columns and girders which made possible the widespread use of glass. Neither material led directly to attempts at originality; the aim was to build a handsome store or office building such as the old Wanamaker-Stewart store in New York, destroyed by a spectacular fire in 1956, or the buildings along lower Market Street in Philadelphia. In residential and modest commercial work fashion looked to the Italian Renaissance; the New York brownstone house owes what distinction it has to its pedimented windows and doorways, not to the chocolate building material.

The classical heritage was not strong enough to restrain the search for the picturesque initiated by the romantic era. Where the style once was found in the villa grounds, it now made its way into the city under the cloak of experiments in the Gothic, Romanesque, Moorish, and other elusive styles. There were so many varieties that they gave rise to a Battle of the Styles, which, by the end of the 1870's, was to leave American architecture completely disorganized. With feverish eagerness many architects set about joining different kinds of ornament or devising new kinds, and in some cities their efforts rivaled the influence of the Second Empire. Oddest of all was the fortress-like work of Henry Hobson Richardson, whose buildings were said to be defensible only in the military sense. His Trinity Church in Boston swayed the profession for more than a decade.

In retrospect it is surprising that the era which was to end in architectural chaos could still boast that the federal government had remained fast to the Jeffersonian tradition of architecture. It was not an accident, but the consequence of the government policy of retaining the leading classical men right down to the 1860's. Charles Bulfinch succeeded Latrobe as architect of the Capitol, which Thomas U. Walter was to complete. Robert Mills did the Treasury Building and the Patent Office and began the Washington Monument in 1848, to be finished by General T. L. Casey in 1884. Ammi Burnham Young became architect to the Treasury in the early 1850's; his work can be found in Boston, Providence, in Norfolk, Virginia, Portland, Maine, and Galveston. Although small in dimension, they achieve a grand scale. He was succeeded by Isaiah Rogers, best known for his hotel work. The hotels have gone, but we still have his Merchants' Exchange, now encased in the main office of the First National City Bank on Wall Street. The strong bond of a continuing tradition resulted in governmental buildings of a pleasing and uniform style.

It is equally surprising to learn that this age also produced the first equestrian statue cast in the country, the Jackson statue in Lafayette Square before the White House, and the first large-scale mural work in the National Capitol. Constantino Brumidi's project in the latter building is still the most extensive of its kind in the country, with its climax, *The Apotheosis of Washington*. It was as if the federal government had declared that fashion could rule where it desired but that, in the matter of its own architecture, only the classical tradition could convey the majesty it demanded. The one exception in Washington was the Smithsonian Institution, the lamentable pseudo-Gothic error on the Mall.

It was the thread of the classical, kept alive by the government, which the archi-

*The first equestrian statue in the country stands in Lafayette Square, Washington. General Andrew Jackson by Clark Mills, 1853. The one in Jackson Square, New Orleans, is a copy.*

tects of the next generation would take up and give such strength that the country found itself in the American Renaissance.

## THE AMERICAN RENAISSANCE

The Battle of the Styles, with the picturesque in the lead, was not to end suddenly. If, on the one hand, many brownstone houses in New York had excellent classical detail, many were picturesque and New Yorkers continued to tolerate the wretched building material, anti-classical in its poverty. In church architecture Richardson's megalithic Romanesque spread beyond the confines of Boston and found its way into profane work, notably private houses and office buildings. The wealthy, who enjoyed a more important role than they do today in matters of fashion, did not seem to care what architectural confection they were served. As for the architect, his presence on the scene was hardly noticed. Only in 1858 did Richard Morris Hunt win a suit against a client over the matter of fees, and the prestige of the architect at last began to be established in America. People turned casually to the architect, if they turned to him at all. Men of money and ambition were satisfied with curious, if sometimes large, houses like the one, now the Manhattan Club, that Leonard W. Jerome built for himself on Madison Square in New York. The grandfather of Sir Winston Churchill obviously confined his pleasures to horses, yachts, and visits to Europe.

It was a client of Jerome, William Kissam Vanderbilt, grandson of the commodore, who ordered a design of Richard Morris Hunt which was to transform American architecture. For the private palace on Fifth Avenue Hunt turned to the French Renaissance for inspiration, not in the Second Empire version but at its source, in the chateaux of the Loire Valley. It was the first of the many great houses which were to make the avenue the cynosure of elegance. No detail was neglected, no effort wasted, no money spared to make it far and away the most spectacular building of its kind in the country. The skill and care were not lost on other architects. Charles Follen McKim would often walk up the avenue in the evening to admire it, saying that he slept better for the sight of it, and, having gazed on it, he was ready to go home for another cigar before retiring. The delicacy and sureness of its execution was a new sight for Americans, and a standard was set from which there was no retreat until our own time.

The Vanderbilt house which formerly stood at the northwest corner of Fifth Avenue and Fifty-second Street has gone—it was torn down in 1924—but another, built in 1885, remains to convey what Hunt had started. A block away on Madison Avenue rises the group of Villard houses. The U-shape plan takes a whole block front on the avenue and has a court of honor, in itself something new to the American scene, but, more important, McKim, Mead & White gave this group of private houses the uniform façade of an Italian Renaissance palace. Its only fault, and it is a serious one, is the material used—brownstone. If the firm had never done another building, this effort would have been sufficient to make it known. The excellence of the interiors, with work by Augustus Saint-Gaudens, still reminds us of the revolution Hunt had begun when he decided to rival the best of the past. No wonder Americans began to look at their architects for the first time and recognize in them the artists who would challenge the world.

Each new palace meant new splendor. As we glance back, it is astonishing to see what was accomplished in several decades. By 1900 the American townscape was taking on a distinction which unfortunately it is now losing. Only Newport remains relatively untouched, witness of what was done in those days.

Before turning to the other triumphs of the American Renaissance we must see how the change was brought about. As with most transformations it was the result of long preparation. The key to the style was the discovery of the École des Beaux Arts by Americans. A number of circumstances led the widow of the Honorable Jonathan Hunt, member of the House of Representatives from Vermont, to take her family to Europe. Not least was her determination to give the two eldest boys, Richard Morris and William Morris Hunt, the best that Europe had to offer in the way of schooling in the arts, and the best was to be found in Paris. When Richard enrolled at the École des Beaux Arts in 1846, American architecture took its first important step away from provincialism. Five years later he left the school to travel over Europe and Egypt. In 1854 he entered the office of Victor Lefuel, his master at the school and architect in charge of the extension of the Louvre under Napoleon III. His position under Lefuel was important enough for him to be responsible for the design of one addition, but his success, and the pressure of French friends, did not stop him from returning home in 1855.

Putting aside his native intelligence and peculiar genius, one may well consider what he underwent in Paris. He had spent five years at the school, working in an atelier, attending lectures, studying the works of art in the city about him, and even indulging in sculpture under Antoine Barye, the best animal sculptor of the century. The Beaux Arts curriculum was a systematized version of the classical training of the previous centuries, fitted to the educational pattern of the time. It was conducted in ateliers, that is to say, studios of groups of students working under a leading architect accredited to the school. The studies and problems were prescribed by the school administration and carried out, not only under the critical eye of the master, but also under that of other students. In a sense it was largely a form of co-operative education in which the older hands taught the younger. The student advanced by obtaining points awarded on the basis of merit and competition. In addition there were lectures to attend on architectural history, architectural theory, building legislation, physics, decorative composition, etc. There was nothing to equal it at home, nor anywhere else, for that matter. The first American architectural school was established in 1865 by the Massachusetts Institute of Technology, and it was not until after the First World War that the schools were able to rival the École.

Americans had to study hard, and, although there was no tuition fee, some were so poor they had to support themselves by working on the side, as did Richardson and Augustus Saint-Gaudens. It was no *vie de Bohème* or Left Bank existence of the 1920's for them. The men of the American Renaissance may have lived handsomely when success came later on in life, but most of them had known exacting years in Paris.

Beyond the curriculum was the school's building and their associations. The superb library, the museum of casts, the copies of great paintings, as well as authentic works of art, are not to be found today in any other art school. The visitor can come on all of Michelangelo's important statues cheek by jowl; although they are executed in plaster, the sight is fascinating. And beyond the school is Paris, with its monuments, its museums, and its endless vistas, sufficient to satisfy the visual hunger of any ambitious student. We know that Louis Sullivan, who rebelled against the dominant aim of the school, respected its qualities and discipline. Principles and standards of design were the lesson of the French school, with many examples at hand to point to. Its training, then the model for Europe, proved a most valuable one in qualities and skills common to all architecture. Based on the study of the classical orders, it cultivated a perception of proportion and a relation of adjustment and scale, that is to say, a sobriety, measure, and understanding which set the educated architect apart from the uneducated. If the work of a graduate was sometimes commonplace or monotonous, it was never illiterate, and it discouraged the temptation to lapse into the vulgarity of trying to be original for originality's sake.

One of the influences of the École caused the founding of new architectural schools in America and the improvement of old ones, especially after 1890. Here the Paris-trained men, sometimes Frenchmen, had a key role. In 1894 the Society of Beaux Arts Architects began to establish "ateliers" and "*concours*" (competitions) of "*projets,*" in imitation, and this instruction led to a new profession. In all this the leaders, men like Charles Follen McKim and Thomas Hastings, had a direct part. The climax of the effort was the creation of the American Academy in Rome, with its Rome Prize awards in imitation of the French Academy there.

The great men ranged beyond the confines of architecture; they cultivated all the arts in the Renaissance manner. That Hunt would turn to sculpture was typical, and anyone who has seen the sketches of the Beaux Arts students will recognize the importance they gave to knowing how to draw. Some of McKim's sketches have distinction of their own. Still another contribution of the French education was the enjoyment of the past and its treasures. The curiosity of the Beaux Arts men and those they influenced was wide-ranging, always keeping an eye for some object or other, and assembling collections which have since found their way into museums. They turned aside to help painters and sculptors. We think of Hunt singling out a seventeen-year-old Austrian shortly after his arrival in New York, the immigrant boy who was to become the well-known Karl Bitter. Or Thomas Hastings helping Raffaele J. Menconi and Paul W. Bartlett, or Stanford White designing the base of the statue of Nathan Hale (in New York's City Hall Park) by the then-unknown Frederick MacMonnies. Mural painting found a place in American art at last, thanks in large part to the commissions obtained with the aid of George B. Post. Henry Ogden Avery, an associate of Hunt and a product of the École, was responsible for the great architectural library at Columbia University which now bears his name.

Last, and not least, the great school tied architecture to city planning. In its philosophy the highest achievement was not the single building but a complex of buildings, a fact which the greatest American planner, Daniel H. Burnham of Chicago, always recognized. The Beaux Arts architects saw problems in terms of the *grand projet,* or grand design, which students of the École had to do when competing for the Prix de Rome. (We must remember that the school is known on its emblem as the *Scholae Augustae.*) Restricted to French nationals, to be sure, the competition in the form of designs fifteen feet by fifteen, with elevation and plan, encouraged a conception of architecture which was bound to influence the American students. The "Paris men," as they came to be called, returned home with a vision of the city which had not existed since Jefferson.

The École had one very serious fault, a fault which was part of French archi-

"The Red Badge of Courage" *could well serve as title for this heroic group representing the Union Army by Frederick W. MacMonnies, 1898. It is part of the Soldiers and Sailors Memorial Arch in Brooklyn's Grand Army Plaza. It is about the best of its kind in the country. The spandrel figure is by Philip Martiny. (J. B. Bayley)*

tecture from about 1800 on. It was preoccupied with the so-called "rationalism" or, as we would put it, "functionalism." Not all the ateliers in the school nourished the false theory, but its influence was strong and in tolerating it the school betrayed the French classical tradition. When the first Americans came back from Paris, this "rationalism" was in their baggage, notably in the case of Hunt and Richardson. It was the great virtue of Hunt that he put it behind him when he came to design the William Kissam Vanderbilt house. McKim, Mead & White, who had known the Richardsonian "rationalism," now followed Hunt's lead to design the Villard houses and the Boston Public Library with a classical hand. Americans were asserting their independence of the École by following the French to Rome, the golden source, and they returned to America to go forward to a new classical which existed nowhere else in the world at the time. With the World's Columbian Exposition of Chicago in 1893 the independence which comes from being steeped in the past was declared in triumph and in consequence the "Paris men" far surpassed their French colleagues in the mistress art.

In 1891 the leaders of the American Renaissance assembled in Chicago at the invitation of Daniel H. Burnham. Many of them, including Burnham himself, had toyed with the picturesque; all but Louis Sullivan were to consecrate themselves to the classical after the fair. By common consent Hunt was given the place of honor; his Administration Building dominated the exposition skyline with its dome. The assembled designers, only a minority of whom had actually been at the École, although they were all trained in its spirit, were welded together to work in one style, and they knew exactly what they were about.

Henry van Brunt, trained by Hunt and one of the men of the fair, explained at the time what they had in mind. His observations are quoted at length because they form one of the most important declarations of faith in the annals of American art and one which has been entirely neglected. "In view of the fact that these buildings had a mutual dependence much more marked than any others on the grounds [he was referring to the structures around the Court of Honor, the fair's main feature], and that the formal or architectural character of the court absolutely required a perfect harmony of feeling among the five structures which inclose it, it became immediately evident to these gentlemen that they must adopt, not only a uniform and ceremonious style—a style evolved from, and expressive of, the highest civilizations in history—in which each one could express himself with fluency, but also a common module of dimension. These considerations seemed to forbid the use of medieval, or any other form of romantic, archaeological or picturesque art. The style should be distinctly secular and pompous, restrained from license by historical authority, and organized by academical discipline. It was not difficult, therefore, to agree upon the use of Roman classic forms, correctly and loyally interpreted, but permitting variations suggested not only by the Italians, but by other masters of the Renaissance. It was considered that a series of pure classic models, in each case contrasting in character according to the personal equation of the architect, and according to the practical conditions to be accommodated in each, but uniform in respect to scale and language of form, all set forth with the utmost amount of luxury and opulence of decoration permitted by the best usage, and on a theatre of almost unprecedented magnitude, would present to the profession here an object-lesson so impressive of the practical value of architectural scholarship and of strict subordination to the formulas of the schools, that it would serve as a timely corrective to the national tendency to experiments in design . . . To such it is hoped that these great models, inspired as they have been by a profound respect for the masters of classic art, will prove such a revelation that they [the architects] will learn at last that true architecture cannot be based on undisciplined invention, illiterate originality, or, indeed, upon any audacity of ignorance . . . It may fairly be anticipated that the great palaces of the court will illustrate the vital principal of unity in variety on a scale never before attempted in modern times."

The illustration conquered beyond their wildest hopes. Only Louis Sullivan saw the attempt as evil and he simply could not understand what was being done. He lived long enough to mark the exposition with a curse which Modernists forever delight in parroting, and it is about time that the record be set straight. A wiser judgment came from Henry Adams, who, as a great historian, had the breadth of view to see what had been achieved. "The Exposition itself defied philosophy," was his observation. "One might find fault till the last gate closed, one could still explain nothing that needed explanation. As a scenic display, Paris had never approached it, but the inconceivable scenic display consisted in its being there at all ... The first astonishment became greater every day. That the Exposition should be a natural growth and product of the Northwest offered a step in evolution to startle Darwin; but that it should be anything else seemed an idea more startling still; and even granting it were not—admitting it to be a sort of industrial speculative growth and product of the Beaux Arts artistically induced to pass the summer on the shore of Lake Michigan—could it be made to seem at home? Was the American made to seem at home in it? Honestly, he had the air of enjoying it as though it were all his own; he felt it was good; he was proud of it; for the most part, he acted as though he had passed his life in landscape gardening and architectural decoration. If he had not done it himself, he had known how to get it done to suit him, as he knew how to get his wives and daughters dressed at Worth's and Paquin's. Perhaps he could not do it again; the next time he would want to do it himself and would show his own faults; but for the moment he seemed to have leaped directly from Corinth and Syracuse and Venice, over the heads of London and New York, to impose classical standards on plastic Chicago. Critics had no trouble criticising the classicism, but all trading cities have always shown traders' taste, and to the stern purist of religious faith, no art was thinner than Venetian Gothic. All traders' taste smelt of bric-à-brac; Chicago tried at least to give her taste a look of unity."

*A classical post office in Laramie, Wyoming, by James Knox Taylor, 1905. It is a typical example of style brought to all parts of the land by the American Renaissance.*

And at the end of his soliloquy he announced: "Chicago was the first expression of American thought as a unity; one must start there."

Even before the fair the American Renaissance had shown the promise of the future in its drive toward the unity of a classical standard. It had not been confined to private palaces. There was first of all the completion of the Washington Monument, a gigantic obelisk set in the middle of the nation's capital. The Statue of Liberty, erected in 1886, was a staggering example sent from France; here, for the first time since ancient Rome, a true colossus had been built, placed in an unrivaled setting. The enthusiasm that greeted Stanford White's Washington Arch in New York in 1889 was a foreshadowing of what was to come. Made permanent three years later, it was joined by one of the few rostral columns in the country, the one which stands in Columbus Circle, also in New York, on the celebration of the explorer's discovery of America. For the same occasion the lampposts devised by Richard Rodgers Bowker were placed along Fifth Avenue from Washington Square to Fifty-ninth Street, and the avenue was decorated with bunting by Stanford White. The Chicago exposition was, in a sense, as much a climax as it was the beginning which Adams divined.

By the 1900's the transformation of American cities was well under way. It involved individual buildings, to be sure, but, as their designers belonged to the same school and appreciated each other's aims, unity appeared in the townscape. After the private palaces came the clubs, the apartment houses, the railroad stations, the office buildings, the banks, the churches, the state capitols, the municipal buildings, and the city plans. In civic design the City Beautiful Movement appeared. The first part of this book has offered the reader some notion of the wealth in New York, but a walk in any American community reveals the bounty of the American Renaissance. And, again, if those who want originality must have it, they will find it in all categories of buildings from country houses to city halls. The splendor of the buildings built in the 1900's surpass their European equivalents in most instances. Paris can point to the Grand and Petit Palais and the Alexander III Bridge, London to the Royal Automobile Club, the Ritz, and the London County Council Building, but there is little else. The lobby of the American office building glittered with marble ornament, a clubhouse commanded the street scene as would a Roman palace, the bank interior made its European equivalent look like a cigar store. Even the flagpole base and the lamppost had moments of glory. The clustered towers of lower Manhattan gain their power because they are, for the most part, classical. Movie theaters, perhaps the last full expression of the American Renaissance, were among the more elaborate products of the age.

In civic design there is less evidence, for too few of the many projects of the City Beautiful were carried out, but the example of the approaches to the Manhattan Bridge in New York gives us some notion of the breadth of the designer's dream. At one end there are piers with rostra, serving as settings for symbolic statues by Daniel Chester French, at the other a triumphal arch with colonnades. In Chicago one part of Burnham's plan of 1909 was completed, that portion where Michigan

*The interior of the great waiting room of the Union Station in Chicago. Designed in 1926 by the firm of Graham, Anderson, Probst & White, the architectural heirs of Daniel H. Burnham, it is one of the important monumental interiors in the country, an excellent example of what the men of the American Renaissance achieved. (Chicago Architectural Photographing Co.)*

*Columns and cornices, obelisks and balustrades accent the setbacks of a classical skyscraper. The tripod at the summit of the air-borne pyramid serves as a steam outlet; steam floats above it in winter, giving the impression of incense burning. The former Standard Oil Company Building at 26 Broadway, Carrère & Hastings, architects, Shreve & Lamb, associates, 1922. (J. B. Bayley)*

Avenue crosses the Chicago River; there is no more spectacular grouping in the country than this mixture of river, boulevards, bridge and skyscrapers. New York placed the Grand Central Terminal and the New York Central Building astride

Park Avenue, creating a new concept in the history of civic design. The national capital is the best example by far of what the taste of the age was able to accomplish. It had been a sorry sight at the end of the century; little had been done since the Civil War. The efforts of Burnham, McKim, Saint-Gaudens, F. L. Olmsted, Cass Gilbert, and others helped to make it the beautiful city we know today.

Organizations such as the Architectural League of New York flourished, holding exhibitions of nationwide importance where all the arts were represented. If the reader would leaf through the catalogues of the League exhibitions, he would be astonished at the extent and quality of the work. It is not surprising that the first tapestry factory in the country was opened in New York in 1893 and that there were three going strong fifteen years later. Municipal art societies were founded all over the country with the aim of improving the city. They gave prizes for plans, lamppost designs, and murals, and they held exhibitions of civic design which were milestones in the history of American art.

From the grand conception to the smallest bit of ornament buildings were designed and executed with care. Knowledge held no terror; the scholar's and artist's hands were one and the same. If some of the buildings did not attain the full impact, it is possibly due to the absence of statues, of adequate murals, or of fine materials. The Pennsylvania Station in New York has an interior which, as monumental as it is, could be improved by statues and murals, and the detail of the ceiling should be repaired and picked out in gold. Patriotic statues, such as marble replicas of great statues of our presidents, Houdon's Washington, Saint-Gaudens' Lincoln, David d'Angers' Jefferson, and others could easily be placed about the main concourse. Some buildings have excellent ornament, as in the instance of McKim's University Club and Whitney Warren's New York Central Building. The latter is admirable; one detail has a winged wheel set against a cloud and sunburst of stone to remind us that a railroad corporation has its headquarters here. The classical ornament to be found everywhere in the country, be it a Houston bank or in Denver's Civic Center, is one of the neglected awards for the traveler's eye, and we can be thankful that there was such wholesale borrowing from the past. Masks, fretwork, rinceaux, gadroons, cut-rolled-leather patterns, egg-and-dart molding, and even Gothic detail bring our buildings to life, something the Modern has failed to do. Gothic ornament, not easy to handle, is wonderfully employed in the Woolworth Building in New York, the Tribune Tower in Chicago, and the Cathedral of Learning in Pittsburgh. In the last-named, which houses the University of Pittsburgh, there is an immense Gothic hall which is breath-taking.

The list of achievements runs on. The American Renaissance appeared at one point like an eternal cornucopia, forever pouring forth new wonders. To the men who led the school the tide of it appeared endless. "When you get through with your work on the other side and come home ready to build, you will find opportunities awaiting you that no other country has offered in modern times," was the promise held out by McKim to Lawrence Grant White, the son of his lamented partner, about to finish his studies at the Beaux Arts. "The scale is Roman and it will have to be sustained . . . Enough has been done to assure the development of

83

*Gothic ornament, freely treated, serves to accent the soaring height of Chicago's most beautiful skyscraper. The Chicago* Tribune *Building, designed in 1922 by Raymond Hood and John Mead Howells. (Kaufmann & Fabry Co. Courtesy the* Chicago Tribune*)*

the future City of Washington along the lines of School 'projects' . . . The best of it is that Uncle Sam is now proud of what is being done and is going to demand the very best that millions can purchase; and there is no fear of falling back into the desperate order of things which has heretofore always existed. Mr. Hunt was the pioneer and ice-breaker who paved the way for recognition of the profession by the public; and now his successors are paving the way for 'vous autres!' who are to come home and design the *really great works*." There was nothing to cloud McKim's optimism. Even San Francisco's Panama Pacific International Exposition was in the offing, the last of the great scenic displays of plaster architecture, to take place in 1915. Some of the triumphs have been touched on, and they were to continue through the 1920's. Related aspects, such as the advance in mechanical equipment of buildings, the improvement in landscape design, improvement in quality and increase in variety of building materials, and the wide range of domestic architecture, gave added tempo to the work being done.

It was the age when mural painting and sculpture especially in public buildings were in honor. The architect accepted them as part of the fabric; the capitol buildings of Minnesota, Iowa, Wisconsin, and Pennsylvania have them both in quantity. Business saw matters in the same light. It was no accident that Benjamin Wistar Morris made place for the mural and stucco designs of Ezra Winter and Barry

*A pool, an orangery, and a terrace complement this villa in the Bronx, New York. The Anthony Campagna residence (1929), by Dwight James Baum, architect, and Brinckerhoff, Vitale & Geiffert, landscape architects. (Gottscho-Schleisner)*

*Goddesses and a god in the heavens seen through a baroque arch with seated giants below. A portion of the* trompe-l'oeil *mural by Allyn Cox in the entrance hall of the William A. Clark Library (1926), University of California at Los Angeles. Robert Farquhar, architect.*

Faulkner in the Cunard Building in lower Manhattan. A palatial hall of travertine has domes, semidomes, and walls which are covered by the painter. Robert Farquhar offered an equally warm welcome in the William A. Clark Library in Los Angeles to the work of Allyn Cox. A large mural salutes the visitor on the threshold. Above a marble-lined hall gods and goddesses disport in cloud-filled heavens seen through open baroque arches. Below them, lolling on cornucopias, are giants guarding niches which contain symbols of the arts and sciences. Here on a coved ceiling are false perspective, skillfully devised architecture, graceful figures, the human form as few can do it today. Paul Valéry said that the triumph of the artist was to place ten or more figures in a setting and have them live and breathe, and this Allyn Cox has done.

Beyond, a high-ceilinged music room looks out on a wide lawn. A large canvas graces the wall at each end and above are many more, set in the most elaborately carved wood ceiling in the country. Masks, garlands of fruit, fluttering ribbons, cut-rolled-leather work weave intricate frames about the canvases. The pictures vary in size, the larger ones depicting scenes from the story of Anthony and Cleopatra as told in Dryden's *All for Love,* the smaller ones symbolic figures, and still smaller ones scenes from ancient legends. Except for the smallest, in grisaille, they are painted in bright Venetian colors which distinguish the work in the hall.

In the garden art the classical was introduced by Charles Adams Platt in the Brandegee estate in Brookline outside of Boston, now the seat of the American Academy of Arts and Sciences. In 1897 terraces, formal bedding, pergolas, and other ornaments were placed about the house, announcing a new kind of landscape. Many others followed, notably the gardens of Jacques Gréber formerly found outside of New York and Philadelphia. One of the best in that of Villa Viz-

*The lavish garden of Villa Vizcaya (1914–17) looks out on Biscayne Bay, Miami. Designed in the Italian manner by F. Burrall Hoffman, Paul Chalfin, and Diego Suarez, it is now part of the Dade County Museum. (Wayne Andrews)*

caya, now the home of the Dade County Museum, outside of Miami. F. Burall Hoffman, Paul Chalfin, and Diego Suarez produced one of the most lavish in the country in the Italian manner, Suarez being the chief designer. There are others like the many-terraced grounds of the Hearst Castle at San Simeon, which, with its palace, forms a superb complex; it is the public's good fortune that the heirs of William Randolph Hearst have seen fit to turn the estate over to the state of California. Or there is the garden, on a more modest level, of the William Wallace, Jr., villa in Hillsborough, also in California. Here green walls of Monterey pine border terraces, statues fill green niches, formal parterres and a pool complete the rest.

For all the transformations and triumphs the Roman scale was not sustained as McKim had expected. In the 1930's the American Renaissance faded rapidly, save in government architecture, and the Modern superstition dominated. The last great monument was the National Gallery of Art, completed in 1940 on the designs of John Russell Pope. Its central hall would have delighted his old teacher, McKim. The walls are of Alabama rockwood stone, the floor composed of green marble from Vermont and gray marble from Tennessee, while the columns about are of dark green marble from Lucca. Giovanni da Bologna's Mercury stands in the center above a fountain; the sculptor who knew splendor of another Renaissance might be somewhat awed by the setting here given his statue.

With the 1930's the flood of Picturesque Secessionism rose to swamp the nation. Only here and there are occasional islands, work of men who have had the courage to stand by their convictions with clients who have not been swayed from beauty's demands. Their contributions are modest perhaps, for they have been denied the big commissions, but they are not to be judged by the customary yardstick of success. They are far more important than is generally acknowledged be-

*The rotunda of the National Gallery of Art with the fountain surmounted by Giovanni da Bologna's bronze figure of Mercury. John Russell Pope, architect, Otto Eggers and Daniel Paul Higgins, associates, 1938. (Courtesy National Gallery of Art, Washington, D.C.)*

cause they and their work are little known. Many Americans desire the classical, even though the Secessionists would drive it from the land. Not until the supporters of the traditional have a vehicle will they know how many allies they have or how many buildings are to their credit.

We have noted the work of Frederic Rhinelander King earlier. And there are the many residences of Mott B. Schmidt and Victor Proetz. William and Geoffrey Platt follow in the steps of their father, Charles Adams Platt; the Stern house in New Orleans is among the best of their work. Page Cross has looked to the class-

The Stern residence (1940) in New Orleans is a good example of the persistence of the classical. The architects William and Geoffrey Platt were prompted in their design by the local Louisiana tradition. (Gottscho-Schleisner)

Roman Ionic pilasters rest on a wainscoting and support a simple entablature. The doorway has a pediment resting on brackets in the shape of volutes. A good example of current classical work done in 1956, it is the board room of the America Fore Loyalty Group, 80 Maiden Lane, New York. Page Cross, architect. (Louis Reens, Courtesy Cross & Son)

*A cottage on Cape Cod designed by Page Cross in 1955. The architect has submitted to the local manner in making use of weather-beaten shingle and clapboard with white trim. It is typical of the classical approach in its ease and adaptability. (Louis Reens, courtesy Cross & Son)*

ical in decorating the directors' room of the America Fore Loyalty Group of New York and given the setting a combination of dignity, repose, and elegance found too seldom nowadays. For a cottage recently built on Cape Cod he has followed a local tradition with walls of unpainted shingle and clapboard relieved by white trim; it is typical of the continuing satisfaction that the traditional offers even in modest structures and, in parenthesis, it is much more difficult to achieve success in this than most people realize. Richard Koch and Samuel Wilson, Jr., have placed a small porch with Tuscan columns and pediment on the R. S. Taggert residence in Crosby, Mississippi. It caps the effort which was spent on the brickwork, the slate roof, and the many-paned windows, contributing a pleasing touch to the whole. Even abroad there are signs of stirring when men like Sir Albert E. Richardson, former president of the Royal Academy, battle for the classical, or when Émile Terry of Paris designs a sumptuous classical theater for Charles de Beistegui in the Chateau de Groussay, now recognized as one of the most beautiful projects recently executed in France.

90

*Richard Koch and Samuel Wilson, Jr., embellish with a handsome porch the R. S. Taggart residence, built in 1957 in Crosby, Mississippi. The classical tradition continues in all parts of the country. (Richard Koch)*

For the majority of architects, and it is also true of their clients, especially among businessmen, Secessionism has won the day. "Perhaps he could not do it again," Henry Adams had warned of the businessman at the Chicago fair; "the next time he would want to do it himself and would show his faults." The prophecy would be too true if we were to say that the American is insisting today "to do it himself" in terms of denying the help of the past. In the Chicago fair his architects had "a profound respect for the masters of classic art," as Van Brunt put it, and knew "that true architecture cannot be based on undisciplined invention, illiterate originality, or, indeed, upon any audacity of ignorance .." Adams's warning proved of no avail.

If there are reasons for despair, there are reasons for hope. For one thing Picturesque Secessionism contains within itself the seed of its own destruction; on another count the splendor of our classical past offers too much of an attraction not to influence us again. Before taking leave of the American Renaissance we might invite a cheerful note and dwell on two grand designs now forgotten.

91

Daniel H. Burnham had pointed out the superiority of an "orderly and fitting arrangement of many buildings" over the virtues of a single building. The great Chicago architect drew from his experience at the Chicago fair and his work on the Chicago Plan of 1909. Whitney Warren achieved the quality in his Grand Central Terminal and New York Central Building, a group still surrounded by complimentary buildings. Yet there are two others to consider. The name of Arthur Brown, Jr., means little to anyone outside of San Francisco and Paris; even in his native city his work has been neglected, and yet he was one of our greatest artists. Born in Oakland in 1874, he attended the University of California. While studying engineering there he was encouraged to look to architecture by Bernard Maybeck, a great artist in his own right, who urged him to go to the École des Beaux Arts. From 1897 to 1901 he attended the famous school, a member of the atelier of Victor Laloux, the outstanding French architect at the turn of the century. Brown's genius found quick recognition, for he became his master's favorite pupil. In fact his success was such that he was discouraged from entering the school competitions because he won inevitably. Not long after his graduation he returned to San Francisco and entered into partnership with a Beaux Arts colleague, John Bakewell, Jr. Their great opportunity came in 1912, when they won the competition for the San Francisco City Hall. They were to know other victories, notably the Pasadena City Hall, but their most outstanding remained that of San Francisco. In 1932 Brown, together with G. Albert Lansburgh, did the War Memorial Opera House and the War Veterans Memorial Building to form the heart of America's greatest civic center.

It is best to approach the wonder from the west, that is to say by the entrance of state as would the fashionable opera lover. We enter a court guarded by tall railings of blue and gold wrought iron and proceed past the Opera House and Veterans Memorial Building through another grille also of blue and gold. The pile that confronts us is a large rectangular building made imposing by a colonnade of Roman Doric, while pedimented and columned porches set off the wings. Above, set on a columned drum, rises the great dome crowned with a lantern. Everywhere our visual hunger is fed with a wealth of detail. A pair of blue and gold lanterns ornament the terrace, elaborate gold-on-gold doors set off the entrances. Bowed Atlantes hold the central balcony on their shoulders, masks resting on cornucopias adorn the keystones, the wrought-iron railing of the balcony presents gold lions' heads and swirling acanthus leaves, the high-columned porch carries a pediment filled with figures—Wisdom stands centrally among the Arts, Learning, Truth, Industry, and Labor. On entering we traverse a stately vestibule and corridors until we stand in the great hall beneath the dome. Four massive piers rise up to four pendentives which spread and join to form a ring; upon it stand composite columns supporting a coffered dome with an oculus, which opens on another inner dome bearing the city's arms surrounded by a chaplet of trophies.

High composite pilasters mark the main story of the hall, which, on its west and east sides, rises to a high barrel vault shallow in depth, and from its floor spills a flight of stairs, like a stately glacier, spreading gently as it touches the ground. Again there is the superb detail, the bas-reliefs in the spandrels, the masks and

*The greatest architectural ensemble in America, the War Veterans Memorial Building left, and War Memorial Opera House, right (1932) Arthur Brown, Jr., and G. Albert Lansburgh. In the center stands the City Hall of San Francisco (1912–15), by John Bakewell, Jr., and Arthur Brown, Jr. Thomas Church laid out the formal court. (Moulin Studios, San Francisco)*

garlands in the semidomes over doorways, the figures beneath the barrel vaults, the bronze work of the lamps, the bronze and ironwork of the railings. (For some of this work Bakewell & Brown were indebted to a French colleague, Jean-Louis Bourgeois, who was killed in the First World War.) In the just quantity of ornament, in the play of space, in the total overwhelming effect, the San Francisco City Hall is the best that American art has produced.

*Interior of the San Francisco City Hall, showing the great stairway and the columned entrance which leads to the Chamber of the Board of Supervisors. With its profusion of ornament in stone, stucco, and wrought iron it is architecturally the most magnificent interior in America.*

*The porch of the Interdepartmental Auditorium (1932) by Arthur Brown, Jr. The sculpture in the pediment is by Edgar Walter. The open galleries to either side separate the auditorium from Labor on the left and Interstate Commerce Commission on the right. They and the porch are worthy to serve as background for some future Titian, Veronese or Tintoretto. A building that has few peers, it bears the stamp of Brown in the columns, the keystones, the lanterns, and the general boldness of the design.*

San Francisco's contribution need not blind us to the second grand design. Again the hand of Arthur Brown, Jr., has lingered, this time in Washington. The magnificent façade which stretches from Twelfth to Fourteenth Streets along Constitution Avenue is his, binding the Interstate Commerce Commission and Department of Labor buildings with the Interdepartmental Auditorium. It would be difficult not to recognize the golden lanterns, the bold masks, the entasis of the columns, and even more, the appointments of the interior as the work of Arthur Brown. The auditorium, next to the Rotunda of the National Capitol and the hall of John Russell Pope's Archives Building, is the outstanding interior in Washington. Brown's use of classical detail and his insistence on gold join to astonish. Everywhere there is an impression of luxury and order and tranquil power.

*The main portion of the Post Office Building façade on the Twelfth Street Circle, which forms part of one of America's grand designs. Designed by William Adams Delano of Delano & Aldrich in 1928 and completed in 1932, it is, with its arcade and shape, too rare a sample of civic embellishment. The sculpture in the pediment is by A. A. Weinmann.*

To the west, on Fourteenth Street, is Commerce, whose design is due to Louis Ayres of York & Sawyer, and on the east the Post Office Building of William Adams Delano of Delano & Aldrich. The three mark three sides of the Great Plaza, today a parking lot punctuated with booths for parking attendants and untidy trees; in its unfinished condition—for the fourth side on Pennsylvania Avenue is missing—it is a revelation of the neglect which has killed monumental Washington. The Great Plaza is the only square of its kind in the country and, despite its present disposition, one of which the nation should be proud.

Arthur Brown does not hold the stage here as he does in San Francisco. His work bows on one side to that of Ayres in the Commerce Building. Of the three architects Ayres was the one responsible for fixing the cornice height at 105 feet and for choosing orange-red tile of the roofs. Brown's effort also bows to that of Delano on the right, the Post Office Building, which has the place of honor at the center. Delano recognized his advantage by giving his building on the Great Plaza side a giant exedra set off at the ends of columned porches; it conveys the sense of distinction and nobility that fixes the tone of the square. There is yet another open space on the other (east) side of Delano's building, this time a circle. Again it is the only example of its kind in the country and an arcaded circle at that, with a curved pedimented porch in the center of one half. In the other half Louis A. Simon of Washington adopted Delano's façade for his Internal Revenue Building, unfortunately only part completed.

It is well to pause on this grand design, which forms part of the "Triangle," that group of government buildings bound on one side by Constitution Avenue, on the second by Pennsylvania Avenue, and on a third by Fifteenth Street. In the late 1920's, on the initiative of Andrew W. Mellon, then Secretary of the Treasury, plans were laid for the city's improvement. To this end he appointed as his consulting architect the late Edward H. Bennett of Chicago. Bennett, a Beaux Arts

*An air view of the western portion of the Triangle in Washington, D.C. The buildings from lower right to center left are: Justice, Internal Revenue, Post Office, Interstate Commerce Commission, Interdepartmental Auditorium (with porch and high pediment) and Labor with Commerce at right angles to Labor. On the hither side of the Post Office Building, the one with the hour-glass shape, can be seen the Twelfth Street Circle, on the other side is the Great Plaza. The National Museum and the Mall are in the foreground and in the center background the White House. (Fairchild Aerial Surveys, Inc.)*

man, had worked with Burnham on the 1909 Chicago Plan and through Burnham provided the link to the Chicago fair of 1893. With Bennett as chairman a committee of architects was formed in 1927, counting Arthur Brown, Jr., William Adams Delano, Louis A. Simon, Milton B. Medary (of Philadelphia), and Louis Ayres, with John Russell Pope of National Gallery fame joining later. They laid out the plan of the Triangle and in the manner of the men of the Chicago fair, fixed the cornice height and agreed on the over-all style, the high classical. As Mellon put it, they "intended these buildings, while having each a separate and distinctive architectural treatment, shall be of harmonious design and grouped around two large interior courts or plazas somewhat after the arrangement of the Louvre in Paris."

The choice buildings fell to Ayres, Brown, and Delano. Ayres was a product of the great days of McKim, Mead & White, a firm that ranked next to the École des Beaux Arts as a training ground for architects before 1914. Delano, like Brown, came from the atelier of Victor Laloux. It was Brown, the elder of the two, who helped him prepare for the school; the two men went their separate ways on graduating, one West and the other East, to join in Washington in carrying out in stone the projects they had done on paper in Paris.

The two grand designs came to an end as the curtain was being drawn on the American Renaissance, and they have been confined to oblivion by the Secessionists. Brown, who took part in both, failed to obtain recognition in this country and yet in 1926 he succeeded John Singer Sargent as corresponding member of the Académie des Beaux Arts of the Institut de France. He died in 1957.

When the Golden City rises in the next decade, it will spring from the work of the men of the American Renaissance, above all from that of Arthur Brown, Jr.

# CHAPTER FOUR

# The Golden City

IN SPITE of the triumphs of the American Renaissance the daemonic forces of abstract nihilism prevailed. The men who made the classical contribution had approached the Golden City, but somehow too many of them accepted it casually. Fond parents, with some misgivings, they handed their patrimony to their successors as Apollo gave the reins of the sun chariot to Phaëthon and fashion raged unbridled as nature uncontrolled. To them it could not seem possible that the classical would not endure, any more than the chariot of the sun would leave its course, and some of them who have seen it go down stand bewildered at the spectacle. It is hard to believe that the heirs of Alexander Johnston Cassatt and Samuel Rea at the helm of the Pennsylvania Railroad would place the visual canker of the new ticket booths in one of McKim's proudest efforts and yet such has come to pass. The chariot of fashion has long since abandoned the classical path of taste and now it brings destruction on every side.

We think of gutted Park Avenue or the new lamppost of the New York street, an open razor gashing the sky, or of the rude entrance to a new apartment house. Small towns have been as much the victims as large cities. A charming crossroads such as that of Rhinebeck on the Hudson is made waste by an ungainly gas station. The countryside has been spoiled for the eye. It is not only the approaches of our cities, such as at Denver, where the highways are lined with chaos and ugliness; it is out in the fields and the woods. Liber and gracious Ceres, fauns and dryad girls, and the great god Pan have fled before man's insensibility. We exploit our countryside as the angler who put aside his rod for explosives. Into the American landscape go explosives of the expanding community, and havoc rules.

As we blandly go about our business, we blame the urban and rural chaos on the automobile, the super-highway, the real estate subdivision, and speculation. A glance at our history would remind us that this has happened before, especially when the great railroad network threaded its way through the land, but with the American Renaissance the City Beautiful tamed the steam engine. The New York Central System covered its Manhattan tracks to create the magnificent terminal and Park Avenue; Chicago, on beholding Burnham's plan, brought order to its riverbanks and Michigan Avenue. Orderly communities arose on the outskirts of cities guided by the artist; some of them were given squares with uniform architectural treatment, one of the best being that of Lake Forest by Howard Van Doren Shaw. But when the automobile and the super-highway were to appear on the scene in our time, the chariot of art was already in reckless hands, the lessons of the past were being derided, and we were not prepared for the future's growth and expansion.

The city had held the center of the stage in the American Renaissance, and to it the artists had given their best, from churches to civic centers. It was the inevitable consequence of the unity Chicago initiated in 1893. Nor was it an accident that in the countryside beauty was nourished, both by the landscape architect and the conservationist. The first real attempt to preserve our great natural resources in forest and scenery occurred in the 1900's under Theodore Roosevelt.

The classical image embraces all in its frame. It was this hated image, with the city at its center, that our false prophets and our Phaëthons have abused, and they succeeded in destroying it by the time the forces of material expansion were in the land. Yet they believe that they can answer the problem with suggestions of merging city and country, of breaking up the metropolis into fragments of small cities and subsistence homesteads, a world so jejune that it would condemn us forever to the setting of soap operas.

Some Secessionists accept the growing urban complex and dying landscape as part of present existence. They praise the rapidly changing scene for its invention and display of energy, its dynamism, as something essentially American. There is as much unreality in the acceptance of the urban sprawl for the city of the future —Los Angeles is an oft-cited example—as in turning to soap-opera solutions. It is not unlike the approach of so many contemporary painters to life when they offer disorder to the beholder on the one hand or sketchiness on the other. To pass from a gallery filled with abstract pictures and caricatures, the work of men who have never dared to commit themselves, into one filled with classical work is to know relief. Here is the substance we are seeking, which we call *reality*, the reality of human existence. It is the world of men and women, all flesh, blood, and spirit. It welcomes the Promethean spark and gives savor to the daily ritual. The artist has dared to have an aim, he has peopled his canvas with figures in action, he is telling a story and telling it well.

The question of aim, what we are trying to do, where we are going, is paramount, and we might as well begin there, at the beginning. The aim of America is to build the great democratic society to achieve the good life for all. In its visual form it is the achievement of the classical image in a free world. For that reason Jefferson turned to "Roman taste, genius and magnificence." Our exploits and our triumphs were to be commemorated in classical terms, the conviction made permanent of the worth of the American ideal. It was a bold stroke of L'Enfant to turn to the most royal garden in Europe as model for the capital of a republic; Versailles gave shape to Washington, which was to become the Golden City, the cynosure of the world. No less bold was the adoption of the dome set on a drum as symbol of the democratic state. We have seen how the federal government held to the classical image, refusing to join in stylistic battles. In the 1880's the extraordinary drive to strengthen the image came when the men from the Beaux Arts

100

saw what had to be done. Chicago's Michigan Avenue, New York's Grand Central complex, the San Francisco Civic Center, and the Great Plaza in Washington were the proudest rewards.

For all Jefferson's dislike of the city he was not afraid to build one; instinctively he saw it at the center of his dream and his reality. It was a city's taste that he offered his countrymen "to reconcile to them the respect of the world and procure them its praise," as he wrote to James Madison. This is the city which is the apotheosis of civilization, where the past, present, and future are joined, where every generation must bring some monument to know immortality. Here are to be found the treasures which moth and rust do not corrupt. Not just any city shape will do, only the classical can give a conscious pattern in the form of a fully articulated plan, the product of unity, which can be accepted in visual terms. Here the city does not reach out to destroy but insists on protecting the countryside, its sacred complement. Order, in plan, prospect, and content is of the essence; the axis, after all, is man's invention, a part of his struggle over the turnings and twistings of nature.

William James is the probable source of the fallacy that busyness with its acceptance of disorder is reality. In defining the nature of his philosophy, pragmatism, he compares it with "the world of concrete personal experiences," that is, the life "in the street"; the traditional philosophical approach, termed "transcendental idealism," he likens to "a kind of marble temple shining on a hill." William James notwithstanding, the marble temple on the hill is as much a part of concrete personal experience as is the life of the street. To destroy the temple is to rob us of aim, and to take away aim is to deny reality with its attendant, morality.

An understanding of it would show us how to transform abandoned Ellis Island, to take one example, into a pleasure ground and a memorial, for reality accepts such a vision no matter how distant it may be. The former immigration center could become part of the excursion to the Statue of Liberty or an accessible retreat where families from both sides of the Hudson might pass a summer's afternoon or evening. Instead we are so blinded that not one imaginative proposal has been offered for its use.

We need the reality which recognizes the hierarchy in civic design, by giving greater importance to places where the public does or might congregate. For that reason government buildings take precedence as foci in the urban scene and offer that sense of identification which binds the community together. Forgotten, or bruised, as they often are today by Secessionist tampering, they invite dejection and indifference. In San Francisco the Civic Center has already been mauled by fumbling Modernists and there is even talk of carrying it further by adding an abstract courthouse. Enough damage has been done already without compounding it. As an alternative Stanford Stevenson, an interested amateur who resides in Berkeley, across the bay, offers a courthouse in the high classical manner for the present parking lot at the southeast corner of the plaza. His façade of high-arched bays is inspired by those of George W. Kelham's library nearby, while the detailing pays compliment to the work of Arthur Brown. Rusticated arched entrances, masked

101

*A proposed new courthouse for San Francisco, by Stanford Stevenson, to complete the Civic Center. Mr. Stevenson, whose role is that of a lively amateur, was prompted to attempt the design by the failure of the Modernists to offer an adequate solution.*

keystones, gold lanterns, and statues are offered in profusion. Fulton Street, between the courthouse and the San Francisco Public Library, is seen as a court of honor with elevated promenades to conceal some ramps lately installed by Modernists. Stevenson suggests a triple row of clipped sycamores, a fountain, vases, and statues as embellishment.

We have seen that, in terms of public use, it has been an American contribution to make temples of their banks and palaces of their railroad stations and department stores, such as Marshall Field's in Chicago. Splendor once reserved for royal residences and noble mansions was brought to the people and it continually sought out new types of buildings for its province. Only today have we given up this tradition. Our housing projects are good examples of our failure. Here we have cities within a city, in several instances communities of twenty-five thousand, and yet the projects have no shape, turn their backs on the communities about them, and have no place in the urban hierarchy. To show the classical answer, John Barrington Bayley has designed a housing project for the western end of 125th Street in the center of Harlem. The main thoroughfare of one of the city's more famous quarters needs a setting of distinction, one which will pay compliment to the Hudson River nearby as well as to the city. He has set his buildings on formal lines around a central point, the focus in this instance being an equestrian statue of General Grant. Monumental façades are joined by arches and take the form of exedras to convey a sense of grandeur, embracing the streets and inviting the people to enter instead of forming walls to exclude them. Furthermore he has designed it to accommodate families on more than one income level. His is a truly democratic solution in the Roman spirit, where people of different means can live and meet instead of the public-housing ghetto or the residential subdivisions based

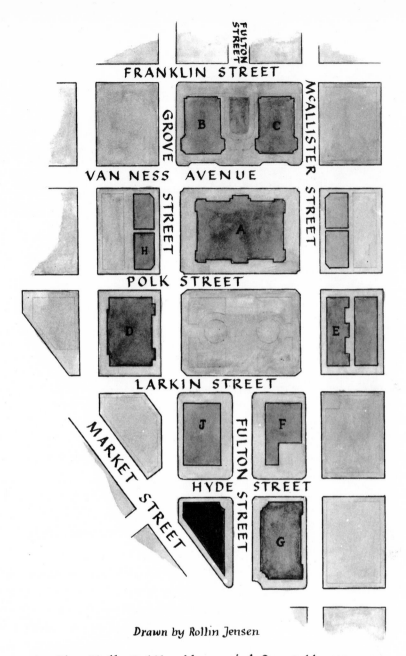

Drawn by Rollin Jensen

A. City Hall · B. War Memorial Opera House
C. War Veterans Memorial Building · D. Civic
Auditorium · E. State Building · F. Public Library
G. Federal Building · H. Health Center · J. Proposed
New Courthouse by Stanford Stevenson

*The plan of the Civic Center of San Francisco, showing the location of its main buildings as well as that of the courthouse proposed by Stanford Stevenson. Courtesy Rollin Jensen.*

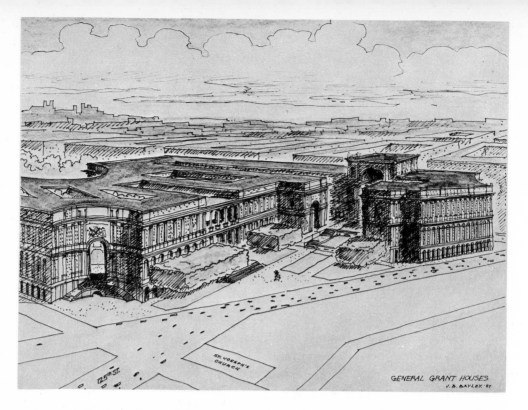

A perspective from the northeast of a large public-housing project for the foot of 125th Street in Harlem, New York City. (BELOW) *its plot plan. Both by John Barrington Bayley.*

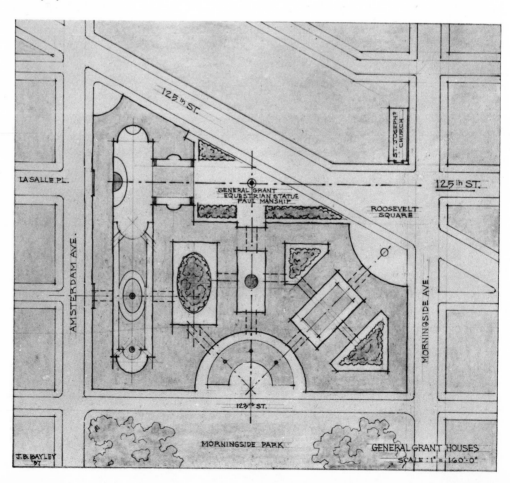

on income level. In housing projects it would permit shops, drugstores, bars, news-stands and other amenities. Such flexibility and freedom, so much a part of the classical, are simply not part of the current vocabulary.

There are many chinks in the hierarchy of the urban scene. The squares, plazas, circles, and parks are too rare; one can go for blocks without finding a statue or a simple monument and in most cities triumphal arches, rostral columns, and just plain columns are wanting. Strangest of all in a nation which loves music, the dance, the theater, and opera is the glaring absence of places to shelter the performing arts. For every million of population there should be a grand opera house, for every half million a ballet or light-opera theater, for every quarter million a municipal repertory theater with a permanent company. The few that have been built follow the example of the Shed at Lenox and the few that have been inherited are becoming fewer, what with the opera house in Boston being torn down to make way for a parking lot. Above all, our national capital has no grand opera house or great theaters. It is incredible that they do not exist in a city which shares the power to rule the destinies of the world. No other fact reveals to what degree reality in the arts is a shadow today, and yet we can hardly blame our statesmen for hesitating to shelter the performing arts when the only contemporary solution is Secessionist.

To meet this need and, at the same time, to allay the fears of our public officials, several New York architects and the author are ambitious enough to present classical answers. Following the author's suggestions, Charles Thompson has done a design showing the completion of the Great Plaza of Delano, Brown, and Ayres. On its north side there is a building to compliment Brown's work opposite, and in it there is a national repertory theater. It is a mistake to allow a beautiful square to go to waste as a parking lot; that can be placed underground. It should be converted into a formal garden, as was originally intended; two double rows of clipped small-leaf European linden would go along the sides, while down the center would be a *boulingrin* or a sunken parterre of boxwood embroidery with pomegranate and orange trees set about in tubs and beds of flowers changed according to season, such as tulips in the spring and chrysanthemums in the fall. (The planting follows the suggestion of Mrs. Margarett Sargent McKean of Pride's Crossing.) Statues would be placed about, twelve representing the twelve months of the Shepherd's Calendar or a number representing the rivers of America or the states. Along the allees of linden would be copies of the great classical works, the Dying Gaul, Venus Anadyomene, Diana the Huntress, the Medici Venus, Silenus and the child Bacchus, etc. The national theater on its exterior would follow the lines laid down by Brown, except that it would have an arcade with round-arched bays and in the center at the second story an open colonnaded gallery as in the Commerce Building nearby. Along the arcade we have shops, refreshment stands, and bars, while in the clement season the wide gravel swath between the building and the linden row would have tables, chairs, and umbrellas. The capital is without a public place where the millions of visitors can rest and take their ease; an oasis is here provided in the nation's most magnificent square. The theater has a state entrance in the form of an exedra on Fourteenth Street, and inside is a grand lobby

105

*A view of the Great Plaza and the Twelfth Street Circle in the Triangle in Washington, showing the building for the proposed new National Theater, as conceived by the author and drawn by Charles Thompson. To the right is the completed Circle of William Adams Delano, which would house the Teatro Olimpico, as a new memorial to Thomas Jefferson.*

and stairway which leads to a hall of mirrors and gold running within the second-story gallery. For the decoration of the auditorium the source of inspiration is the recently restored theater of Versailles; where there the curtain has gold fleurs-de-lis on a blue ground, here gold eagles are set on a blue ground. The remainder of the building is given over to apartments, studios, and other facilities for the members of the repertory company and the apprentices of its school.

Today the square is wasted at night as it is during the day. We must picture it with the great theater, on the evening of a state performance in spring. The presidential cavalcade moves along Fourteenth Street to the exedra entrance, bright lights are everywhere and possibly fireworks, an orchestra is playing in the plaza, and crowds stroll along the paths, stand to listen to the music, or pass under the arcade.

At present our most imperial street is in a sad state. Pennsylvania Avenue is unfinished and must be completed to serve as a *via triumphalis* from the White House to the Capitol. We suggest that monumental façades be constructed on the north side of the avenue by the government; these will be sold to the present owners or future owners on condition that the façades remain unchanged. What the owners

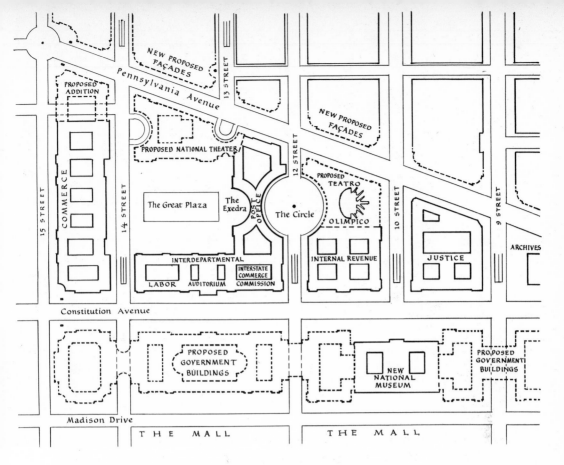

*Plan of the Triangle Area in Washington by Charles Thompson and the author. It shows the creation of monumental Pennsylvania and Constitution avenues lined with continuing façades of the same height to be carried out in the classical manner.*

build behind the façades will be entirely up to them. In the same fashion additions will be made to the present buildings across the avenue to fill the lacunae of the continuing line of buildings and the pattern repeated on the south side of another triumphal way, Constitution Avenue, where a line of connected buildings will include the National Museum and the National Gallery. The buildings, as in the instance of those on the north side of Pennsylvania Avenue, will be joined by handsomely ornamented arches.

The author takes the liberty of appending to the Thompson scheme a second, more modest theater, which will be placed in the yet unfinished portion of the Internal Revenue Building of Louis A. Simon. Delano's Circle on Twelfth Street will be completed, and behind the façade the public will come on an imitation of Palladio's Teatro Olimpico in Vicenza. This pleasant invention accommodates one thousand two hundred; the viewers will have before them the image of the classical city as the great Vicentine architect saw it. Ancient drama, chamber music, and choral singing will have for their residence another memorial to Thomas Jefferson whose genius roamed the arts. The state entrance will be on the Circle, for as in the instance of the Great Plaza it is too precious not to be given life by night as well as by day.

107

*The Teatro Olimpico in Vicenza. Designed in 1578 by Andrea Palladio and completed in 1584 by Scamozzi. The permanent stage is Palladio's attempt to reconstruct an ancient Roman theater. (Vejenti, courtesy Ente Provinciale per il Turismo di Vicenza)*

Supreme among the future embellishments of Washington is the National Grand Opera House. Its designer, who prefers anonymity, has placed it east of the Capitol Building in the center of a rectangular plaza built parallel to the Capitol. The opera house fits in the east side of the square facing the Capitol, which will be seen through an opening on the west side. The conception will prove particularly effective at night when the opera lovers assemble in the square or wander out on the high-columned open gallery of the *piano nobile,* for they will have before them the famous dome brightly lighted. No traffic will be permitted in the square except the cavalcades of state; ordinary traffic will be gorged beneath the complex. It will be the refuge of the sight-seer or stroller, who will have large fountains to reward him together with the decoration of the buildings. The opera house has two monumental colonnades which form the semicircular sides of the square; from these, palatial blocks stretch out towards the Capitol. The blocks will have uniform façades, arcaded, columned, and adorned with sculpture in the ancient Roman manner. Like the Great Plaza it is another oasis offered the foot sore tourist. As for the auditorium and proscenium the architect has taken his cue from the San Carlo Opera House of Naples.

Returning to New York, Bayley suggests a baroque opera house for the city. A striking improvement to Columbus Circle offers the needed springboard to action. A colossal portico with enclosed galleries surrounds the Circle, left free-stand-

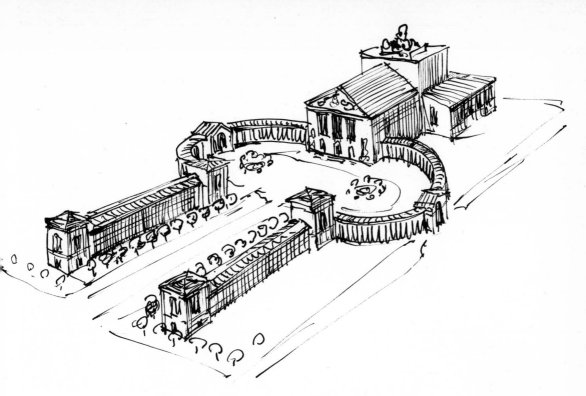

*A perspective of the proposed new National Grand Opera House set in its square, east of the National Capitol. A monumental colonnade shapes the plaza, from which extend two palatial arms which contain offices, apartments, and shops. The whole is sumptuously adorned with sculpture.*

ing on the Central Park side while on the other side concealing, among other unfortunate structures, the ugly New York Coliseum. It is joined to a concert hall and the opera house by a grand stairway in the manner of Bernini. From there we enter a high-domed foyer, then to a magnificent oval stairwell, and last to the auditorium. Taking its inspiration from the present opera house auditorium by Carrère & Hastings, ornament sits splendidly, with gold and red the predominating colors. Before us rises a proscenium framed by Solomonic columns and topped by figures bearing the escutcheons of the city, state, and nation. Overhead a dome peopled with many figures blazes with a sunburst.

We cannot leave the above buildings without dwelling on the iconography, as much a part of reality as the human figure. (For all its importance there has not been a public building constructed since the war where story-telling has its place.) Stevenson's San Francisco courthouse provides ample room for the artist to shower his gifts. The iconography here will revolve around Justice and the Law, and the themes will be found in world history as well as the history of California. In Bayley's housing project local history and national history can be intertwined in the decoration, supplementing the presence of the equestrian statue. The statues of our heroes and the story of our country are part and parcel of the classical. It is one of the wonders of our National Capitol to come on so much history in canvas, fresco, and stone, whether it is Houdon's portrait of Washington, John Trumbull's large

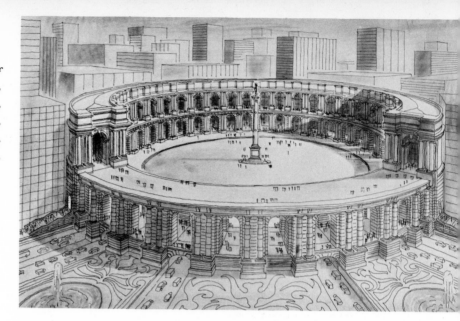

*Perspective of the proposed new Columbus Circle in New York with the Grand Opera House and concert hall by John Barrington Bayley. It shows the pedestrian, or forum level.*

*Interior view of the great Reception Hall of the rebuilt Columbus Circle complex by John Barrington Bayley. A view up the Golden Stairway to the rostral column of the present Columbus Monument.*

*Interior of the Great Gallery of the Columbus Circle complex. The design is inspired by the Hall of Mirrors of Versailles. John Barrington Bayley, inv.*

*The interior of the auditorium of New York's Grand Opera House, designed by John Barrington Bayley.*

canvases, or the halls and committee rooms where Constantino Brumidi evokes the many facets of America in murals.

The new opera houses and theaters offer equal opportunity to display the ancient tales and legends. The National Grand Opera House has the theme of Aphrodite bringing the arts to Washington. Aphrodite, *"Aeneadum genetrix, hominum divumque voluptas"* (Mother of the tribe of Aeneas [or Rome], delight of men and gods), as Lucretius hailed her, will be seen coming up the Potomac on a conch shell whiter than ivory with wheels of gold. Drawn by white horses with flaming eyes and foaming mouths, it leaves a broad wake, while around it dolphins rise and fall and tritons circle blowing conch shells. Above her, carrying the various symbols of the arts, winged cherubs and little zephyrs gambol. In a corner Aeolus let through the sun and blue sky to restrain menacing clouds and dark forces. The dome holds the main picture; elsewhere there are scenes from Aphrodite's life, her birth from a wave near Crete, her nightly bathing in the Peneus, her acceptance of the apple from Paris. Her symbols will decorate the building, that is, the rose, the cockleshell, the myrtle, the swan, and even the lowly sparrow. In Thompson's

111

theater the theme is the birth of the Muses, the meeting of Mnemosyne, or memory, and Zeus in the form of a shepherd. Different tales about them will appear in the decoration: The Muses being led by Apollo, their patron, or *Musagetes,* how the daughters of Pierus challenged them in music and, on being defeated, were changed into magpies, the scene showing them judging the contest between Apollo and Marsyas, and the meeting of Apollo and Calliope, Muse of eloquence and heroic poetry, and the coming of their son, Orpheus. Bayley's opera house has Apollo and his legend. We must picture the sun god, preceded by Aurora, going with his chariot through the heavens of the dome of the auditorium. About the building we will find stories from his life, his birth on the island of Delos, how he killed Python, his unrewarded love for Daphne, and her transformation into a laurel tree, how he slew the Cyclops, etc. His symbols will also be there, the griffon, the cock, the grasshopper, the olive, the laurel, and the palm. Nor will his role as healer be forgotten.

The iconography has been touched on at length to show how absent it is today. By peopling our public buildings with visual history we make them more real, by offering allegories in the form of the stories of the gods we personify the arts. So much for the profane. For sacred stories and allegories the churches have provided and will provide the necessary shelter; it is enough to walk into any museum save a Modern one to see what they once commissioned.

Such canvases and statues cannot be offered haphazardly; they must have "their space, their well-defined light, their subject matter and their federations," to repeat Paul Valéry, settings and frames to accent their beauty and give them permanence. Only ornament can answer their needs. In truth, there is no beauty without ornament, from a molding to a representation of the human form. The variety of it alone delights us and is endlessly rewarding. It is a fact that a bare structure can be taken in at a glance, but an ornamented one invites reflection and beckons to the observer to return and consider it afresh, as does the Mercury motioning an invitation above the Grand Central Terminal. For that reason a classical building, like a symphony by Beethoven, is a series of discoveries. Bits of ornament escape us, as do musical phrases, only to be found on closer familiarity. It gives substance to the play of light and shade and marks by its shadows the sun's daily progress across the sky. A building without ornament, said George Santayana, is like the heaven without stars. And an architecture without ornament is no architecture at all.

It is the absence of ornament in the Modern city which most betrays its unreality. The real world is not a desert, unpeopled and solitary; the real world is full of life and of the reminders of life. ("I plead for decoration," Clifton Fadiman has written, "man is an ornamenting animal.") An essential part of it is reflected in the ornament about us, from the dolphin-headed coffee spout at the Automat to the Statue of Liberty in the harbor. There is no charlatanry here about the "truth" or "integrity of materials," nor a mystique of texture which denies the human touch, nor the abstract substitute for figurative patterns. From ornament we draw immense visual pleasure, life-enhancing as well as life-reflecting.

*O douce volupté, sans qui dès notre enfance,*
*Le vivre et le mourir nous deviendraient égaux*

wrote La Fontaine. O sweet sensuous pleasure, runs the poet's conceit, without which, from childhood on, the business of living and dying would be just the same. Classical art, being objective, is perforce a public art and can answer the general visual hunger; Picturesque Secessionism, being subjective, is private and reserves what small pleasure it has for the few. The first duty of the artist is not in "expressing himself" but in decorating buildings, streets, and squares for the public's visual pleasure. It is by means of decoration that a building is made complete as a work of art. Further, the artist has a moral purpose in revealing our history and religion, portraying our heroes, evoking our poetry, and symbolizing our aspirations. "Art should dedicate itself to the decoration of churches, public places and courts of justice," was the observation of Ingres, and "that is its true and only aim."

In the same way we will welcome the past with its note of permanence. None of us need shrink from the "laughing acanthus" dear to Virgil or the thousand other inherited devices portraying man and nature. We can join with Washington Alston in accepting the old masters as part of daily life. "The artist," wrote that remarkable American, "must needs owe much to the living, and more to the dead, who are virtually his companions, inasmuch as through their works they still live to our sympathies." Michelangelo always maintained that he was an humble plagiarist of the ancients and, when asked what he intended to do in his design for St. Peter's, he said that he would place the Pantheon on top of the Basilica of Maxentius. Gabriel, when at work on the Place de la Concorde, observed that he was only aping the age of Louis XIV. And we have seen what Jefferson did when it came to the design of the Virginia Capitol at Richmond.

If we glance again at our classical past, two features stand out again, the column and the human form. The column would be meaningless did it not take the shape of the Five Orders, the Doric, Ionic, Corinthian, Composite, and the Tuscan. They are the beginning of architecture, they impose the manner and give the measure of ornament, they are the main contribution of our Graeco-Roman heritage. No greater satisfaction is afforded than from the classical column in its work. It is an element of apparent support, clothing a steel member in the great hall of the Pennsylvania Station or as an element of decoration at the top of a skyscraper, as in the old Standard Oil Building on lower Broadway or again in the New York Central Building on Park Avenue, where Whitney Warren has them resting arrogantly on corbels with nothing below them except the city street. Too often men have boasted that a child can design one; all he need do, they say, is to turn to an architectural pattern book and copy. If men like McKim, Warren, Thomas Hastings, and Arthur Brown, Jr., outpace their colleagues, the reason lies in their ability to handle the column, the most difficult component of architecture. What is more, their success or failure, like the painter of a large figurative mural, is easily revealed because their efforts are judged ruthlessly by comparison with past triumphs. As to the human figure, which holds such terror for the Modernist, it is everywhere present in the classical. In painting and sculpture it is present in its obvious aspect; in architecture it is seen always in relation to ornament. A third facet of its role has been defined by Geoffrey Scott, who saw that the classical had as "its method, to transcribe in stone the body's favourite states; and the moods of the spirit took visible shape along its borders, power and laughter, strength and terror and calm. To have chosen these nobly, and defined them clearly, are the two marks of classical style. Ancient architecture excels in perfect definition; Renaissance architecture in the width and courage of its choice." The classical of the future must carry both to a universal application to build the Golden City.

Blessed are we that our classical heritage has not all been destroyed by the Secessionists. Unlike the men of the Renaissance, picking their way through the ruins of ancient Rome, we can go about the land and find buildings entire. If we do have ruins, they are the ruins of the classical canons, that is the controlling principles that must be followed to build in beauty and in the grand manner. For all the debris that has risen about them, they still command. Let us restore them.

The first of these is *composition*. Composition is the ability to join the parts of a building in order to produce a harmonious whole. It means that the work of art must have a beginning, a middle, and an end. The fabric has definite limitation, as a picture in its frame. The alternative is the current glass or concrete grille box. In an architectural composition there are to be found scale, proportion, movement, balance, axis, and unity, all absent in the Modern.

*Scale* is the relation of the parts of a building to the human figure. In achieving scale ornament has a paramount role, offering recognizable parts such as moldings, acanthus leaves, and rustication. A wealth of ornament placed to accent scale allows the eye to measure a building, to find a place to rest, and to attain the security of constant reference. *Proportion* is the search for harmony in the interplay of the principal and the subordinate parts of any visual composition. It invites *movement* or repetition of parts of the structure, especially in the visual detail. By movement the eye is lead to an effect where the repetition is broken. It is a system of reinforcing the accentuation of mass, space, and line. Another element is *balance* in the form of symmetry or asymmetry. It is essential in conveying a sense of repose and in joining groups of buildings, and it helps the observer to know where he stands. The *axis* is an important component of balance. It is the backbone, the formal ordonnance of a plan from which the subordinate parts depend to form an ensemble. In civic design the axis is one of the classical keys, to be found in New York's Park Avenue, or what there is left of it, and in Chicago's La Salle Street. The closing of the axis, as the New York Central Building does Park Avenue or the Board of Trade Building does La Salle Street, is one of the great effects of classical planning. *Unity*, the joining of the parts and the subordination of the parts to form a whole, gives order to a composition and leads to beauty. "The unity which recognizes the distinction [degree of importance] of the parts makes for order," wrote St. Francis de Sales, patron saint of journalism, "and order creates harmony and scale and harmony, in finished whole objects, makes for beauty" and added to these "must be clarity and much splendor in order that the beauty be seen and recognized." Such is the unity achieved in the San Francisco Civic Center.

Then there are the classical elements. We have touched on the first of them, the Five Orders both in column and pilaster. Moldings, in all their variety, are essential. The pedestal, consisting of base, dado, and surbase, is a third. A fourth is the entablature with its architrave, frieze, and cornice. The pediment, both round and triangular, is a fifth. The dome, the arch, the cornice, the keystone, the baluster, the attic, the quoin and rustication are some of the others. They are complemented by the different kinds of ornament: the rosette, the godroom, the volute, the acanthus, the rinceau, the griffon, ad infinitum. Classical America offers examples of them on every side.

Beyond the canons and the elements, classical architecture boasts of certain concepts that make it a federation with the power of assembling all the arts, and they save it from autonomy and loneliness. The first of these is the *façade*. It is the face (façade stems from the same Vulgar Latin word, *facia*) of a building which looks out on the world, and we judge a building by its façade as we judge a man by his face. It has a quality of its own, independent of structure, a certain freedom which permits it to join other façades to create an ensemble. Man does not build for himself alone any more than he smiles for himself alone; the façade is designed out of respect to the beholder, a form of architectural courtesy to the man in the street. An important building in the community demands an important front for the world and the façade answers the need.

What might be termed "façade of the interior" we call *interior decoration*. Again we have the same premise of offering courtesy and conveying a sense of importance. Every room in a building has a quality of its own, and this fact takes on greater importance in buildings frequented by the public. We go into a building by an imposing entrance to find ourselves in an imposing hall and from there we go to a noble chamber, be it in the National Capitol or the San Francisco City Hall. The same devices of columns, pediments, pilasters, sculpture, and painting are found in profusion, all façade to please or impress. A doorway becomes a triumphal arch, not a hole in the wall by which we pass from one room to another, a window is an adornment besides being useful, the walls, ceiling, and floor distract in a pleasing or inspiring fashion. After all, as Milton has told us:

> *Beauty is natures brag, and must be shown*
> *In courts, at feasts, and high solemnities*
> *Where most may wonder at the workmanship;*
> *It is for homely features to keep home,*
> *They had their name thence.*

In the country when we step out of a villa, motel, or bathhouse it will be into a formal landscape. *Landscape architecture* will draw life from our classical past first of all and, if need be, from the picturesque, for the latter belongs in the countryside or in the suburb. Indeed it is in the latter where it has a right to be as Andrew Jackson Downing suggested. In either case the planting will not be left to chance; statues, vases, fountains, pavilions, and other devices will abound, for they make the perspective points and surprises of the landscape. Suburban communities, besides having classical shopping centers filled with art, might welcome a few mossy gods, fountains, and parks. The Country Club District of Kansas City points the way in its shopping center, its parks and fountains. In the city—with the exception of larger parks which will follow the example set by Frederick Law Olmsted and Calvert Vaux in New York's Central Park—the squares and gardens will be formal because they can thus serve more people and offer a place for works of art. Bryant Park, behind the New York Public Library, is a good example, as is Meridian Hill Park in Washington with its long cascade, an instrument of embellishment too seldom used in America. Planting, too, will be formal, with trees cut back and trimmed. While we cut down our forests on every side, we insist on letting trees flourish indiscriminately in our cities. Our latter-day hamadryads have converted Washington into a bowl of salad which obscures the magnificent buildings and much of the sculpture. In the Bishop's Garden of the National Cathedral in the same city the box hedges are allowed to grow to such an extent that it is impossible to go along the paths, and the vista offered is something akin to a burst mattress with green stuffing scattered about. Once the old box is removed, new box should be planted and trimmed to proper shape, and

> *Again the moss-grown terraces to raise*
> *And spread the labyrinth's perplexing maze,*
> *Replace in even lines the ductile yew*
> *And plant again the ancient avenue.*

(Many of the gardens of Virginia suffer the same neglect, when they should be modeled on those of Colonial Williamsburg.)

Not only will our parks and squares have proper ornaments, but the streets will be decorated by beautiful lampposts, traffic lights will have statues (those on Fifth Avenue in New York City are topped by statues of Mercury), and there will even be attractive fire hydrants. Triumphal arches, obelisks, and statues will abound. *Street decoration* was a distinct part of the American Renaissance; it is an integral part of the classical of the future.

With such instruments the artist will attain what he cannot do today, an impression of *monumentality*. Although not essential for private dwellings or commercial structures, it is required by important public buildings. The classical is the style which has successfully brought visual power to man's works by mass, proportion, rhythm, repetition of crucial elements, and by ornament. A hundred-foot cylinder, say a smokestack, is in no way monumental; a hundred-foot Corinthian column is because it has a base, a shaft, and a capital, which is to say, an organization of parts, each with an affirmative character and the parts fitted into a harmoniously assembled whole. The National Capitol attains it by joining a flight of steps, a columned porch, a pediment, a drum and a dome. The skyscrapers of a generation ago obtained their power by having ornament at the eye level or base, with a plain shaft, and ornament at the top or capital. As in all monumental buildings they offer something for everybody to behold; now we look away, for there is no reason to do otherwise. Aspiration, once part of the artist's vocabulary, will return with monumentality.

The Secessionist of today begins his design from a small structural detail or binds it to a trick in the plan, so too Modern city planning is either conceived as a narrow, limited "practical" scheme, obsolete before it is executed, or is based solely on social and economic measures. The classical operates in terms of visual ensembles with a variety of buildings and monuments and offers formal squares and long vistas. All the arts can join to create the effect in civic design as in the individual building. The town and city will become a theater of life with the stage properties made permanent. Its concept is vast as is the luxuriance of its execution, hence it will be called the *Grand Design.* By this name the classical will build the Golden City.

The advent of the classical is not far off, and we would do well to prepare for it. There are clients who demand it and there are men, both artists and artisans, willing to submit to its discipline to meet the demand. It is also very important to realize that the best masonry construction is still cheaper than the new "curtain walls," i.e., "skins" of glass and steel, aluminum or enamel panels. "Economy has not been a factor in most curtain-wall buildings," recently confirmed an authority in the New York *Times;* "masonry and small windows would be cheaper in initial cost and cheaper to air-condition." Cost of construction is then no obstacle in the path of the new classical. But there are steps to be taken. The first is the introduction of the classical into our architectural schools. Today they are *all* Secessionist with the abstract in ascendance. The cult of ignorance, at least in the schools, must come to an end. At the present time the tragedy is that the students are in no way prepared for the inevitable change in fashion; when the classical comes, they will have only the Modern string to their bow, hardly the preparation for a career in architecture. In painting and sculpture the same situation exists; again the traditional disciplines must be placed in honor, with mural painting and public sculpture made the highest aim of the painter and sculptor. It may well be that the schools cannot meet the challenge and there will have to be a return to the apprentice method, where men acquired their art at the drafting board or in the studio of a master. A corollary here is the provision of adequate facilities for the mural painter and the sculptor; in our large cities suitable artist studios are rapidly disappearing. On the public level every city over a hundred thousand must have its cast, copy, and model museum as part of the educational system. Plaster casts or marble replicas of great statues of the world, copies of great paintings, and models of great buildings show the sources of our classical heritage. For purposes of comparison examples of other styles will also be present. One of the few remaining cast museums in the country is that of the Carnegie Institute of Pittsburgh. Fulbright scholars in the arts and pensioners of the American Academy in Rome would have, as their duty, to return with a useful copy or model according to their art, a form of repayment to the American public who sent them abroad. The various artisan trades, such as cabinetmaking, parquetry, wrought-iron work, and other arts, now excluded from the benefits of the Fulbright program, should be permitted to recommend apprentices for awards under the auspices of the AF of L-CIO; the recipients would return with copies of the great examples of their particular craft. Not without reason did the Secessionists destroy or disperse the precious casts, models, and measured drawings when they took over the schools and some museums. Examples of great work might have distracted the students. Goethe, it will be recalled, discovered the classical, after flirting with the Gothic, on first observing a plaster copy of a Corinthian capital from the Pantheon.

The true incentive to the classical lies in patronage, both private and public. When the current Modern is once accepted as out of fashion, as it already is in some circles both here and abroad, when once it is seen in perspective, no one will feel under the obligation to admire or support it. Then the classical will come into its own. Public patronage may very well play the larger role again. "But how is a taste in this beautiful art [architecture] to be formed in our countrymen," Thomas Jefferson wrote to James Madison in 1785, "unless we avail ourselves of every occasion when public buildings are to be erected, of presenting to them models for their study and imitation?" The state of Virginia, the city of New York, and the federal government were but three of the many public patrons who answered him by calling to the arts. The federal government remained one of the leading clients, the outstanding example being the decoration of the National Capitol by Brumidi. In the American Renaissance the painter and sculptor as well as the architect were welcomed by the government. Cass Gilbert, architect of the capitols of Arkansas, Minnesota, and West Virginia and also of the Woolworth Tower, saw public responsibility in Jeffersonian terms: "It has been said that private individuals of modest means can rarely afford to acquire beautiful works of art for their homes, and it is therefore a reasonable function of the State, in the direction of culture and education and in the development of civilization, to provide in the State Capitol, which is owned and used by all the people, a thing of beauty which all the people can enjoy and in which they can take just pride." Our most beautiful opera house, that of San Francisco, was municipally built and is municipally owned. Franklin Delano Roosevelt recognized the government's responsibility to the arts when he set aside work-relief funds for the artist. Our barren government buildings, our new barren embassies and consulates, the United Nations buildings, the Air Force Academy at Colorado Springs are products of a passing fashion, and the day is near when they will be properly adorned by the arts. At present our statesmen, statesmen of other nations, and future leaders of the Air Force must pass important years of their lives in functional sheds; tomorrow these same will be clothed with beauty's raiment.

We must no longer look to the present; our duty lies to the future. The Secessionist has failed for many reasons, but not least because, unable to aspire to the vision of the Golden City, he has never gained solid public support. He cannot grasp the meaning of beauty, which Plotinus knew so well. "It is evident that there is such a quality," wrote the famous third-century philosopher, "perceived at the first glance, recognized by the soul as something long familiar, arresting and beckoning," that physical beauty which looks backward and forward in the same moment, spanning time. The Secessionist cannot weave the golden thread that binds the imagination. We pass on to enter a world so far beyond the horizon of the Modern that it can be forgotten. Reality and beauty, now joined by imagination, touched by the spirit in triumph, reach up to glory to form the classical trinity. It is a sense of glory which overcomes us when we behold the work of art which man has produced on a superb scale. A great American came on this sense as a boy in Paris. Recalling in later life the vision that he first beheld in the Gallery of Apollo in the Louvre, he offers a rare exposition of glory. "We were not aware of style, though on the way to become so, but were aware of mystery, which indeed was one of its forms . . ." The reader may recognize that this is Henry James at the side of his brother, William. ". . . In those beginnings I felt myself most happily cross that bridge over to Style constituted by the wondrous Galerie d'Apollon, drawn out for me as a long but assured initiation and seeming to join with its supreme coved ceiling and inordinately shining parquet a prodigious tube or tunnel through which I inhaled little by little, that is again and again, a general sense of *glory*. [The italics are those of James.] The glory meant ever so many things at once, not only beauty and art and supreme design, but history and fame and power, the world in fine raised to the richest and noblest expression."

We should not be astonished at such an evocation but we are, both at the vision and the word. It is for another age, when there were heroes. Yet we have our heroes today, and every Sunday two thirds of America proclaims the Glory of God in twenty tongues, and even a profane use awaits the word every day to describe the wonders of nature, but beyond God and nature glory seems to have no place. This glory which James knew so well, now denied man and his works, arises from the element of sacrifice. In nature it is bounty on an unparalleled scale, a giant offering of substance and color. For the Christian the glory that is God culminates in the supreme sacrifice of Christ on the Cross and all Christians must accept sacrifice to attain heavenly glory. In other religions, other forms of sacrifice. To the Muhammadan heaven is won by obedience, humility, mercy, and good works, and death on the battlefield. In essence glory is the reward of a form of giving which, despite the accidents of fortune, man must accept to attain a goal.

It is true that when we think of glory we also think of musical instruments and voices joined, the climax of Beethoven's ninth symphony when the chorus breaks into Schiller's hymn, "Alle Menschen werden Brüder . . ." But it is essentially in visual terms that we seek to evoke it. "The heavens declare the glory of God," goes the Nineteenth Psalm, "and the firmament showeth his handy-work," and, to have meaning for us, it must be found in the visual. Leone Battista Alberti, the great Italian architect and humanist, declared that "when we lift up our eyes to heaven, and view the wonderful works of God, we admire Him more for the beauties which we see than for the conveniences which we feel and derive from them." Man makes a sacrifice of effort and skill in embellishing canvas, stone, or metal. By embellishing them he gives them true substance, seeking the sense of permanence which is so much part of reality. His goal is to achieve dignity, invite aspiration, and perhaps attain glory. Man, in this way, reaches upward to the heavens, a striving not disdained by the majesty of God, as St. Augustine reminds us.

The sacrifice of visual glory has its conditions. It demands "a quality so noble and divine, that the whole force of wit and art has been spent to procure it," wrote

Alberti, "and it is but rarely granted to any one, or even to nature herself to produce any thing every way perfect and compleat." Glory will be with us when an awakened public as patron stirs the ashes and revives the fire of classical beauty to a degree unknown in the American Renaissance. Having tasted visual glory more than once in our history, we will taste it again. Josiah Royce believed it not bright enough in the American Renaissance and asserted that it must be part of American life, in the form of "a willingness to sacrifice much in order to put in the form of great institutions, of noble architecture, and of beautiful surroundings an expression of the worth that the community attaches to its own ideals." Only it can satisfy man's natural hunger for aspiration and in its highest form become symbolic of national greatness. We may not follow Louis XIV all the way in his dictum that *"la gloire . . . n'est pas une maîtresse qu'on puisse jamais négligé,"* but glory is a mistress whose demands must be met, particularly today in its peaceful reflection. Among other works of the past that it can point to is the Gallery of Apollo, the first visual proclamation of the age of Louis XIV. The king, it will be recalled, had been nurtured by a prince of the Church, Cardinal Mazarin, and he had before him the image of papal Rome, the Rome of Julius II and Sixtus V. They all knew the vision of Caesar Augustus; the emperor, while keeping the legions at full strength on the empire's borders, found his sweetest joy in the embellishing of Rome. ". . . With justice he gloried (*sit gloriatus*)," runs the famous passage in Suetonius, "that he left as marble what he found as brick." Augustus in turn looked to Pericles, who defended the temples he built for the Athenians. As the state had all the necessities of war, he declared that its added wealth should be put into work to be eternal monuments to the glory of Athens, the Golden City of Greece. In so doing he brought to his people elation, confidence, a sense of elevation, and a loftiness of purpose which overwhelm us even today when we behold the Parthenon.

In a democratic society the Golden City will derive support from many sources. They are the individual, the corporation, the church, the university, and the government. A sign of it may be in a new synagogue or in a private house. There may be a touch of it in a public school building or in a city hall, or it may be the preservation of the countryside. The acanthus that never dies is forever putting forth new leaves. Once initiated, the concept of glory will be found on all sides, seen in the vast framework of classical beauty led by visual splendor and the past. No nation can neglect the arts of peace any more than it can the arts of war, for to do so is to invite disaster. A nation to be great must build its Golden Cities.

# On the Trail of Picturesque Secessionism: a Short History of the Modern Movement in Architecture

### 1. THE ORIGIN OF PICTURESQUE SECESSIONISM

IN THE 1920's, when Modernism began to move beyond the circle of the zealots, it was generally accepted as having no past. The revolutionary tone gave an aura which the most active practitioners were not at a loss to use, but some of the enthusiasts leaned to the respectability offered by history's cloak. Restricting their surveys to obscure figures or touching on a narrow appreciation of the great, they compounded a number of art histories which traced a line of Secessionism to the 1800's. Now that its devotees are comfortably in the saddle, the histories have multiplied and several have even swept Vitruvius and Alberti into their net. For some reason, except for John Summerson's *Heavenly Mansions* they have neglected the giant who looms over the movement, no less a figure than Eugène-Emmanuel Viollet-le Duc.

Among Picturesque Secessionists Frank Lloyd Wright is the only one who has openly admitted to the influence of the Frenchman best known for having restored Notre Dame of Paris, Pierrefonds, and Carcassonne. "Viollet-le-Duc was a teacher of what Dad now calls *organic architecture* as early as 1860," John Lloyd Wright informs us in his book, *My Father Who Is on Earth.* When young Wright asked his father about studying architecture, he received a copy of Viollet-le-Duc's *Discourses.* "In these volumes you will find all the architectural school you will ever need," his father said, pressing the books into his hand. "What you cannot learn from them, you can learn from me," he added. There is another link which Wright has with his French mentor, that of being a highly successful perennial rebel against the classical.

John Lloyd Wright, in leafing through the *Discourses,* came across such familiar expressions as "organism" and "organic," words frequently on his father's lips. If John Ruskin makes use of biological words prior to the famous restorer, he never pronounced them quite so specifically; the emphasis stems from Viollet-le-Duc, to whom Gothic vaulting is "this organism" and the peculiar virtue of Gothic

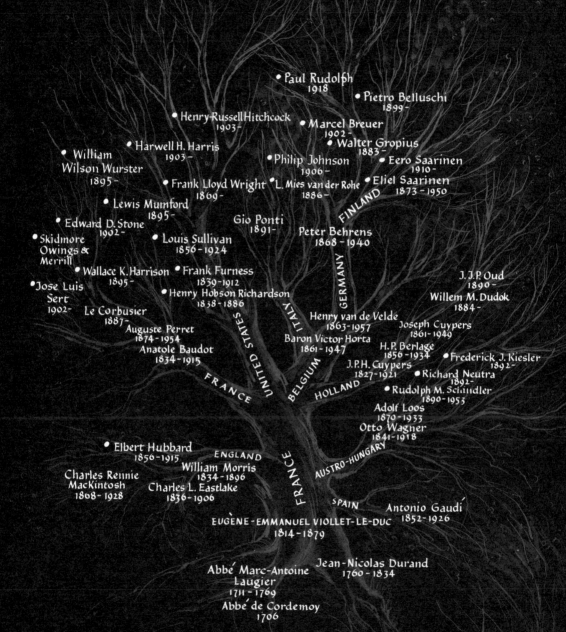

Paul Rudolph
1918

Pietro Belluschi
1899–

Henry-Russell Hitchcock
1903–

Marcel Breuer
1902–

Harwell H. Harris
1903–

Walter Gropius
1883–

William
Wilson Wurster
1895–

Philip Johnson
1906–

Eero Saarinen
1910–

Frank Lloyd Wright
1869–

L. Mies van der Rohe
1886–

Eliel Saarinen
1873–1950

Lewis Mumford
1895–

FINLAND

Edward D. Stone
1902–

Gio Ponti
1891–

Peter Behrens
1868–1940

Skidmore
Owings &
Merrill

Louis Sullivan
1856–1924

Jose Luis
Sert
1902–

Wallace K. Harrison
1895–

Frank Furness
1839–1912

GERMANY

J. J. P. Oud
1890–

Willem M. Dudok
1884–

Henry Hobson Richardson
1838–1886

Le Corbusier
1887–

Henry van de Velde
1863–1957

Joseph Cuypers
1861–1949

ITALY

Auguste Perret
1874–1954

Baron Victor Horta
1861–1947

H. P. Berlage
1856–1934

Frederick J. Kiesler
1892–

Anatole Baudot
1834–1915

J. P. H. Cuypers
1827–1921

Richard Neutra
1892–

UNITED STATES

BELGIUM

HOLLAND

Rudolph M. Schindler
1890–1953

FRANCE

Adolf Loos
1870–1933

Otto Wagner
1841–1918

Elbert Hubbard
1856–1915

ENGLAND

FRANCE

AUSTRO-HUNGARY

Charles Rennie
MacKintosh
1868–1928

William Morris
1834–1896

Charles L. Eastlake
1836–1906

SPAIN

Antonio Gaudí
1852–1926

EUGÈNE-EMMANUEL VIOLLET-LE-DUC
1814–1879

Jean-Nicolas Durand
1760–1834

Abbé Marc-Antoine
Laugier
1711–1769

Abbé de Cordemoy
1706

• Indicates Americans

# THE TREE OF PICTURESQUE SECESSIONISM

construction the fact that "all its organs are necessary and indispensable." Only Wright's "organic architecture," as his son pointed out, is the "rational architecture" which Viollet-le-Duc proclaimed a hundred years ago and which, after a circuitous route, now triumphs in the world. If Wright willingly concedes its importance in his work, no excuse can explain away our easy indifference to his master.

By rational architecture Viollet-le-Duc meant an architecture in which the logic of the plan, construction, and materials dictated the design in the architect's effort to achieve a new and original design, a concept we recognize at once. The mother of architectural invention, according to him, was not imagination but necessity, in the familiar Modern phrase "form follows function." (At this point we cannot help recalling George Santayana's observation that "abundance, not necessity, is the mother of invention.") Within the boundaries set by "reason" the architect must strive to design a building belonging in its place and age, inspired not by the past but by "logic." "Train your judgment, learn to reason, and you will perhaps come to achieve the new," he said. It must be understood that the restorer was applying his "reasoning" power at a very simple level, namely the mechanical. The same holds true for his use of the word "rational." He made architecture out to be a pseudo-science, or a form of "scientism" which is giving science too universal and too "simplistic" an application.

Viollet-le-Duc was hardly the first to have the concept; he only amplified and codified it. Actually it was first suggested by several French churchmen of the eighteenth century. An obscure Canon de Cordemoy wrote a book on architecture in the 1700's hinting at the idea. He was soon overshadowed by the better-known Abbé Marc-Antoine Laugier (1711–69), a member of the Society of Jesus. In his *Essai sur l'architecture* (first edition in 1753, the second in 1755) we find the roots of Secessionism. The fixed principles of art, the Jesuit maintained, could be found in reason and he insisted that "one should put nothing into a building which could not be excused by sound reason," rejecting the visual aspect of the classical. For all his leanings one must not expect a clear-cut definition which might be equivalent of today's functionalism.

Several Italians propounded a similar doctrine about the same time, namely Carlo Lodoli (1690–1761), Francesco Algarotti (1712–64), and Francesco Milizia (1725–98), but none of them enjoyed the popularity of Laugier. No less a figure than Sir John Soane (1752–1837) accepted the Laugier thesis for his lectures on architecture before the students of the Royal Academy in the early 1800's. Numerous copies of the Abbé's work were found in his library at Soane's death, for he was in the habit of passing them among his friends and students. The published inventions of Claude-Nicholas Ledoux (1736–1806)—not his constructed work, which was supremely classical—reflect rationalism in their curious geometric shapes and absence of ornament. In his *L'Architecture considerée sous le rapport de l'art, des moeurs et de la construction* (1804) the main victims appear to be the other arts, notably sculpture, which is almost entirely eliminated.

The mantle of Laugier did not fall to any of these men; rather it went to the great engineer-theorists of the First Empire, one of them being J. N. L. Durand (1760–1834), best known for his large book of plans and elevations drawn to the same scale called familiarly "le grand Durand." He introduced his students at the École Polytechnique, where he was a professor, to the theory and his *Précis des leçons d'architecture* (1801–05) brought it to the attention of a wider public. Here the aim of architecture is none other than "public and private convenience, and the preservation and happiness of individuals, families and society," a worthy end which Alberti had announced in the fifteenth century, but Durand then reduced it by stating that "fitness [function] and economy are the means which architecture must naturally use and they are the source of its principles." Economy for him was no obstacle to beauty; on the contrary its demands are his most fruitful inspiration. He found many to agree with him in dismissing the point of view that architecture is also something decorative, among them Jean-Baptiste Rondelet (1734–1829) who taught at the École des Beaux Arts. Rondelet defended the ideas in his *Traité théorique et pratique de l'art de bâtir* (1802–17), a book which enjoyed considerable success in and outside his country, with six French editions as well as translations into the German and Italian.

Although architectural rationalism had its start at the École Polytechnique, where Rondelet was also professor, it came to lodge within the Beaux Arts, where it had a place beside the traditional study of the Orders, the appreciation of decoration, the acceptance of the past, and the notion of glory as part of the architect's education. The rationalist tinge in France in the first half of the last century came to be known as *Néo-grec,* seen in the tendency to strip the classic of its ornament. Jacques-Ignace Hittorff (1792–1867), the man who was responsible in altering the Place de la Concorde to its present state, shows the influence in his Gare du Nord, one of the Paris railway terminals. So did Henri Labrouste (1801–75), who made use of cast iron and glass in the main reading room of the Bibilothèque Nationale. They did not forget their classical heritage nor did they force the rational argument to the desperate conclusion of today, but they made use of it freely, particularly Labrouste, and some of them left a trail of damage in the great classical buildings they "improved." Labrouste on the one hand, made full use of traditional decoration in some projects and, on the other, he destroyed a beautiful eighteenth-century wing in his glass and cast-iron extention to the National Library. A number of his students outdistanced him in their innovations. In this way, paradoxical as it may seem, rationalism did lodge in the École des Beaux Arts, and our architecture inherited it in part from the much-maligned school.

Although Viollet-le-Duc spent a lifetime in attacking the *Scholae Augustae,* as the school is known on its seal, we must remember that some of the graduates were not quite so far removed from his way of thinking as he would like to have us believe. Antoine de Baudot (1834–1915), architect of St. Jean de Montmartre, precursor of many Modern churches, throws an interesting sidelight on the relation of the early Secessionists to the great prophet. In 1856 Labrouste decided to close his atelier, forcing his students to look elsewhere for instruction. One group of them, following Julien Guadet (1834–1908), author of the famous *Éléments et théories de l'architecture,* chose Julien André (1834–1906), a Beaux Arts rationalist. The other, under De Baudot himself, persuaded Viollet-le-Duc to open an atelier and take them on. In this way the rationalism that stemmed from the Gothic took its place beside the rationalism of the Beaux Arts.

Now for our hero. Eugène-Emmanuel Viollet-le-Duc was born in 1814 to a well-to-do Parisian family, his father being a successful government official and his mother of solid bourgeois stock. He received his education from an uncle, Eugène Delécluze, part journalist, part artist, who counted among his close friends the Romantic Prosper Mérimée, author of *Carmen.* From the start the young Eugène revealed strong artistic leanings—and a rebellious nature. When his family decided that he should go to the École des Beaux Arts, accessible to him through his parents' friendship with Percier and Fontaine (architects who launched the Empire style), he refused to follow their wishes. "You become what others want to make you. The Ecole is a mould for architects," complained the precocious youth at seventeen, "they all come out of it alike." He never changed his mind about the school, and in 1870 he wrote that " a pupil who goes to the École des Beaux Arts is like the poor fellow who gets his finger caught in the gears of a powerful machine, only to find himself drawn through them." Instead he pursued his studies independently and by twenty-one he had obtained his first job as instructor of drawing in a small private school.

Currents of a wider world were sweeping through architecture in these years. The growing importance of science and technology invited interest in structural techniques to the neglect of the decorative aspect. Most important of all was the romantic flood which invaded the arts at this time. Of late the French Revolution has been construed as the source of many contemporary attitudes in art; rather romantic literature, blessing as it did wild nature, the quaint, the obscure, and the distant, transformed the artist's outlook. For example, prior to this time the artist was like anybody else who had a job of work to do, but from the 1830's on he became somebody special, usually recognized by the velvet beret, flowing tie, and beard. The opera *La Bohème* has immortalized this aspect of it. The picturesque element which had been confined to the landscape in the eighteenth century invaded literature, then painting, sculpture, and architecture. The Gothic and the Romanesque, so long neglected, were discovered first by the Germans, later the English, and last the French, who had clung to the classical. The young Viollet-le-Duc came on the Gothic, his lifelong passion, in the company of his uncle and the Romantic Mérimée.

Not long after his first steps in that direction he went to Italy; the voyage only confirmed his inclination for the Gothic and his hatred for all that belonged to the classical tradition except for the Greek, which he looked on as "pure." He simply could not accept the Roman; Rome and its magnificence only discouraged him. His disappointment, it is true, in no way prevented him from drawing everything of interest, for the man's energy knew no rest, but when he returned home it was only to plunge deep into medieval France.

125

Thanks to Mérimée's influence he obtained his appointment in the government department in charge of restoring ancient buildings, chiefly Gothic and Romanesque. "M. Viollet-le-Duc will go to Vézélay and draw the plan of the Church of the Madeleine," runs the instructions dated December 1839, by no less than Mérimée himself, *Inspecteur général des Monuments historiques.* "He will study the condition of the building and make an estimate of the necessary repairs." At the age of twenty-five a career in architectural restoration was launched which has few parallels in history. One great church, cathedral, or castle after another was visited, often with the author of *Carmen,* and one after the other was transformed until half the medieval monuments of France were made new. Notre Dame of Paris, Carcassonne, and Pierrefonds we have mentioned before, but there were the churches and cathedrals of Chartres, Troyes, Sens, Toulouse, Amiens, and Narbonne among the better known.

His observations on restoration are not without interest. "The word and the subject are modern," he wrote in the eighth volume of his *Dictionary of Architecture.* "To restore a building does not mean to maintain, repair or remake it but means to reestablish in a whole state that which can never have existed at any given time." Indeed our own Colonial Williamsburg has been constructed according to his principles of period restoration and it stands with Pierrefonds and Carcassonne as a monument to his inspiration.

It was only one part of the man's work. Mérimée, a close friend of the Countess de Montijo and of her daughter, who became empress, saw to it that he was admitted to the imperial household after 1852. Viollet-le-Duc decorated Notre Dame for the wedding ceremony when Napoleon took Eugénie as bride; he did the same on the occasion of the baptism of the prince imperial. When the court turned for amusement to charades and amateur theatricals, he provided the designs for the costumes and the sets. If their Imperial Majesties went traveling through the country, he accompanied them, penning the court bulletins. Mérimée, who toward the end of his life was confined to a sickbed in Nice, could distinguish those from Viollet-le-Duc's hand by their references to some Romanesque or Gothic monument. He even designed Gothic railway carriages for an imperial train of state.

Under his inspiration old crafts were rediscovered and new techniques in the arts devised. The revival of stained glass is in large part due to his efforts, and Raymond Subes, the leading artist in wrought iron, told the author that Viollet-le-Duc gave life to the art dead since the 1800's. The sculptor Bartholdi, when putting the Statue of Liberty together, turned to a method of handling the copper plates discovered and improved on by the rationalist. The man touched all the arts and some of the sciences in his generation. In the Franco-Prussian War we find him turned military engineer at work on the Paris defenses. In 1875 he entered politics and was chosen deputy for Montmartre. When death finally overcame him in 1879, he had begun an ambitious project on the customs and traditions of France. As John Summerson pointed out, he was one of the giants of the last century.

His greatest monuments were his books. In 1854 appeared the first volume of his monumental *Dictionnaire raisonné de l'architecture française du IXe aux XVIe*

*Water color by Viollet-le-Duc showing the ruined façade of the church of the Madeleine in Vézelay. It was made in 1839 at the command of Prosper Mérimée, author of* Carmen. *(Courtesy Commission des Monuments Historiques)*

*siècle,* and from then to his death the products of his pen and crayon streamed from the presses. Thanks to an easy literary style and to his masterly command of drawing he turned out an unprecedented series of works: The above-mentioned dictionary of architecture in ten volumes, a dictionary of French furniture in six volumes, two volumes of *Discourses,* several architectural books for young people,

127

*Viollet-le-Duc's design for a concert hall in stone, iron, and brick. The structure, as can be seen, is "openly expressed." Note his cipher in the right-hand corner.*

a book on pre-Columbian Mexican architecture, etc. He told Richard Morris Hunt in 1867 that he did all his own illustrating; when it is recalled that there are some six thousand drawings and plans in his books, it is little wonder that he still looms above us today.

His theory of rational architecture, and ours, stems from his structural interpretation of the Gothic. Although we know today that the vaulting of a Gothic cathedral can be built without ribs, to him they were structurally indispensable. The same was true of the pinnacles which contribute so much to our pleasure in the Gothic roof line; "they are destined by their weight," he wrote, "to strengthen the vertical supporting forces." From this false interpretation of the Gothic he reasoned that in all great architecture the form, function, and construction method dictated the design. For him the "aesthetic adventure," as John Summerson has pointed out, was entirely ignored. His own designs, logically conceived from the point of view of construction, plan, and new materials of the 1860's, i.e., glass and iron, were as original as they were ugly; ugliness did not matter, as originality was his aim. In explaining his method of cast-iron construction he observed that, while it is true that what he suggested was contrary to the Greek and the Roman canons, "that must be if we wish to find *the architecture of our epoch* [italics his] which is so loudly called for, that we find it not in mixing past styles but by looking to the principles of new structure." In his interpretation of history he reserved special disdain for the French classical, notably that of the age of Louis XIV. One of his arguments against it was that it was not "original."

Despite the prestige he enjoyed at the court of Napoleon III and despite a band of fanatic disciples he was not accepted as a prophet in his own land. The traditionalists ruled the Académie des Beaux Arts, a division of the Institut de France. The Académie, which saw its duty to maintain taste in classical terms, in turn controlled the École des Beaux Arts and, equally important, the Académie de France, lodged in the Villa Medici in Rome. (The latter institution is far more important to the French than our Academy in Rome is to us; the highest reward the French Government can give the aspiring artist is the famous Prix de Rome; on winning it the student is secure for life in terms of livelihood and commissions.) Many members of the Académie saw Viollet-le-Duc as responsible for the reform of the École carried out in November 1863, a reform by which the government sought the divorce of the École and the Académie, an aim achieved since the last war. (Among the traditionalists on the other side was Ingres.) On top of the attempt which had excited violent passions came Viollet-le-Duc's appointment by the emperor as professor of aesthetics and art at the École on December 6. This proved salt to the academic wound. On January 29, 1864, he appeared on the lecture platform accompanied by Count de Nieuwerkerke, superintendent of the fine arts, Prosper Mérimée, and Théophile Gautier while Sainte-Beuve, the noted essayist, was in the packed hall. "Messieurs," he began, and there he stopped. Yells, shouts, and scraping feet drowned him out. Nieuwerkerke gesticulated frantically, and the response was a shower of apples, eggs, large pennies, and other objects. They stood it for a half hour and then retired before a riotous band of students. Now Nieuwerkerke became the center of attention. His position as lover of Princess Mathilde, the bluestocking cousin of the emperor, was public knowledge and only made for greater uproar.

"*O Ciel! tu sais si Mathilde m'est chère,*" chorused one crew, intoning the famous aria from Rossini's *Guillaume Tell.*

"*A sa Mathilde, ô ciel qu'il coûte cher!*" answered another. Then shouts of "*Ohé! Castor*" broke out, *castor* being the French for beaver. While lost on Nieuwerkerke it was not on others present. The superintendent had lately had a house built for himself and the reference to the beaver was a disrespectful allusion to the animal's legendary building methods. At length the police broke up the demonstration and arrested, among others, Henry Hobson Richardson, the famous Boston architect, then a student at the school. He found himself sharing a cell with

Gautier, who had been picked up by mistake because of his long hair; both were shortly released.

Six other lectures followed under similar conditions until Viollet-le-Duc resigned in disgust despite the pleas of Mérimée, who insisted that he was giving in to his enemies. The official world of architecture was now closed to him. Almost a century later, in 1952, a handsome exhibition of his most famous living disciple paused, while circulating in Europe, at no less a temple than the École Nationale Supérieure des Beaux Arts. Parisians flocked to see the wonders. The ignominy of the master was at last avenged. The irony of the event is that the French, even to this day, have little inkling that Frank Lloyd Wright's ideas are inherited from a countryman.

## 2. THE FIRST AMERICAN PHASE

Not in France but outside its borders did Viollet-le-Duc find his most fervent admirers. Had it not been for the enthusiastic reception of the *Dictionnaire raisonné* in Germany and England, the publisher, it is reported, would have abandoned the project. (An interesting parallel to this exists in painting. Russians, Germans, and Americans were the ones who purchased the work of the Modernists from Cézanne on, not the French. After the last war, for example, the Musée d'Art Moderne in Paris discovered that it did not possess one picture by Georges Rouault.) In the 1850's Georg Gottlob Ungewitter (1820–64), the leading Gothic theorist of Germany, asked his publisher to model his *Gothisches Musterbuch* as nearly as possible on the *Dictionnaire raisonné*. "Viollet-le-Duc," he wrote from Paris in 1859, "has now achieved a very high position and our cathedral master-builders would do well to keep his work before them." The fashion for the medieval in Germany and England, far ahead of France, had long prepared people of both countries for his rational interpretation of the Gothic. In 1855, when the ecclesiastical authorities of Lille held a competition for their new cathedral, fourteen of the forty-one entries were English and Englishmen took the first two prizes, the second going to the well-known Gothic revivalist, George Edmund Street (1824–81). (William Morris [1834–96] was in Street's office at the time; together they went to Lille to see the exhibition of the designs.) Street, in writing of French Gothic, referred his public to the work of Viollet-le-Duc, whose "description of the buildings," said he, "is known already to most of your readers." French Gothic invaded the English scene in the 1860's, strongly influencing Richard Norman Shaw (1831–1912) and others, and in 1863 the restorer obtained England's highest architectural award, the Gold Medal of the Royal Institute of British Architects.

His most fervent English disciple proved to be the architect and critic, Charles Locke Eastlake (1836–1906), not to be confused with his painter uncle of the same name who enjoyed a knighthood. He announced the rationalist theory as a new basis for interior decorating and furniture design. His popular *Hints on Household Taste in Furniture, Upholstery and Other Details* (London 1868; first American edition, 1872) quoted Viollet-le-Duc on the title page. Eastlake told his avid readers that "one of the chief merits of the Pointed Style (Gothic) is that the origin of every decorative feature may be traced to a constructive purpose." Further on, in a statement which might have been lifted *in toto* from the *Discourses,* he maintained that "in the sphere of what is called industrial art, use and beauty are, in theory at least, closely associated . . . No decorative feature can legitimately claim our attention without revealing by its very nature the purpose of the object which it adorns . . ." From the *Hints* sprang the Eastlake style, which was so fashionable in the America of the 1870's, one of the earliest manifestations of Picturesque Secessionism to appear in the country.

The American architect Henry van Brunt (1832–1903), who translated the first volume of the *Discourses* in 1875, offered perhaps the best explanation for the interest in the new theory wherever the Gothic revival was popular. The manner which had originally risen to favor from nationalist and literary inspiration, *viz.* in Germany and England, now had found a "scientific" apologist. "It will be observed," wrote Van Brunt, "as a characteristic of his argument, and as a reassuring fact to the professional reader, that at every step the allurements of mere sentiment, so irresistible to the layman, are distrusted and that the premises of every conclusion claim to practical facts in the arts of building . . . Convictions based upon practical knowledge, gained from experience and observation, even if involving some professional bias or one sidedness, are at least worthy of comparison with theories evolved in the literary manner and subject to the literary temptation of arbitrary statement and sweeping generalization." The rational-functional approach placed all those interested in the Gothic on much surer grounds when they defended it against the assaults of the classical men in the "Battle of the Styles" which raged at the time. Ruskin, the literary source of much Neo-Gothic, later confessed his jealousy on the occasion of the appearance of the *Dictionnaire raisonné.* "I ought to have written it myself," he exclaimed. As far as the professional was concerned, Viollet-le-Duc was a man who spoke his language of construction, but for all the attraction of this aspect of architecture to the nineteenth-century, we can only look on it as pseudo-science. It has not prevented his interpretation of the Gothic from becoming standard: art historians who should know better and industrial designers with literary pretensions still parrot the misconception.

Although Eastlake enjoyed sufficient vogue in this country, it is not to him that we owe our link to the restorer of Notre Dame and Carcassonne. Some may be even disappointed to learn that Richard Morris Hunt was the man who introduced the ideas of the rational point of view to America and set the country on the path of Picturesque Secessionism, a path he himself was later to abandon. (It is for the latter reason that he is not included in the Tree of Picturesque Secessionism.)

With the École offering both the functional and the classical approach, it followed that Hunt came back in 1855 touched in some way by the former. Then the appearance of the first volume of the *Dictionnaire* while he was in Paris was not without effect. A member of the school's staff, Eugène Millet, a friend of Hunt's, confessed once quite openly: "I have had two masters, Labrouste and Viollet-le-Duc. The first showed me how not to do it, the second how to do it." Hippolyte Taine, who succeeded Viollet-le-Duc after the disaster of 1864, hardly differed from him in outlook on many things. His comment on St. Peter's of Rome is typical of the Picturesque Secessionist viewpoint; Wright himself could make the statement. "The vaults, that cupola and the powerful curves, all this apparatus is magnificent and grand," wrote the famous historian of English literature. "And yet there are only two kinds of architecture, the Greek and the Gothic. The others are transformations, deformations or amplifications. The people who built Saint Peter's were pagans who were afraid of being damned, nothing more than that." In the face of such statements from friends and professors of his school Hunt naturally accepted the theories. The buildings of the first half of his career, that is, up to 1879, when he obtained the commission to do the Vanderbilt palace on Fifth Avenue, have a strong Secessionist flavor. A glance at the Tribune Building, still standing on Park Row, or the Stuyvesant Apartment at 140 East Eighteenth Street, both in New York, announce the "honesty" of their design, the emphasis on the mass, the original detail, and the "muscular" quality which betrayed the new manner. Even the small polished-granite columns and their Romanesque capitals on the Tribune Building might have come from one of the master's drawings.

Hunt, as we know, opened an atelier for architectural students in 1858, which a year later had its quarters in his famous Tenth Street Studio Building, torn down in 1956. Among his pupils were James D. Gambrill, (1832–80) later a partner of Henry Hobson Richardson, George B. Post (1837–1913), Henry van Brunt, William R. Ware (1832–1915), and Frank Furness (1839–1912); they must have imbibed Viollet-le-Duc in strong doses, for their work, far more than Hunt's, reflects his influence. It was especially true of Frank Furness in his bank buildings on Chestnut Street and in the Pennsylvania Academy of Fine Arts in Philadelphia. (The latter was designed in collaboration with the Hewitt Brothers.) Van Brunt, as we have seen, translated the first volume of the *Discourses* in 1875, twenty years before both volumes were brought out in England. Hunt himself met Viollet-le-Duc more than once. "The bright spot at this time [1873] was a visit of several days which Richard made to Viollet-le-Duc at Pierrefonds," Mrs. Hunt recalled. "He stayed at a little inn near the chateau, enjoying the congenial companionship immensely." Yet six years later he was to abandon Picturesque Secessionism and lead America to the classical tradition.

His American successor at the École was the much-better-known Henry Hobson Richardson (1838–86). Although he participated in the riot in 1864, he came wholly under rationalist influence. In choosing the Romanesque he was obeying the suggestion of the master who said that inspiration could be found only in a primitive and undeveloped style where construction and architecture could not be separated, it being the way that Western genius revealed its true tendencies and qualities. Richardson, by his picturesque massing and his carefully reasoned search for texture in his materials, won his place as the first true Secessionist in American architecture.

He enjoyed enormous vogue in the 1870's and the 1880's, owing to the popularity of his Trinity Church in Boston. He influenced George B. Post, Charles Follen McKim, Stanford White, and many others in their early years; traces of his

*Old and new Picturesque Secessionism side by side near Independence Hall in Philadelphia. The megalithic pile, formerly a bank, was done by Furness & Hewitt in the 1880's; the glass box by Charles E. Colbert belongs to the 1950's.*

empire can still be found all over the country. For all the prestige it enjoyed at the time of his death in 1886, his was too special a style to last. The movement came into the hands of Louis Sullivan (1856–1924). Sullivan had his first taste of architecture at the Massachusetts Institute of Technology and was for a year in the Frank

*Trinity Church (1874–77) in Boston by Henry Hobson Richardson. An important milestone in the first phase of American Picturesque Secessionism. (Wayne Andrews)*

Furness office in Philadelphia. In 1874 he went to the Beaux Arts, entering the atelier of Émile Vaudremer, a recognized leader among the French rationalists. On his return two years later he was already a fledgling Picturesque Secessionist and he never changed, although in practice he occasionally deviated from his principles. "Form follows function," his famous phrase, may have been the ideal, but it is not always evident in his work. The artist in him insisted on having decoration which has a quality all its own, independent of construction. Further, he was not above designing a façade, as in the instance of the Wainwright Building in St. Louis, where only each alternate column contains a steel shaft, the others being sham. Despite his pronouncement that the chief characteristic of the tall office building was its loftiness and therefore to be emphasized, he continually breaks the lofty effect by offering the beholder a horizontal base, then a vertical slab, and finally a wide horizontal cornice. This mixture does not make his building less pleasing, but it can hardly be termed "logical" or "expressive." His Secessionism is seen best in his conscious attempt to devise a new kind of ornament, "organic" because he was inspired by plant forms. The ornament, like Richardson's Romanesque, was too personal to be handed on and it died with him. His influence lies more in his writings, which were rediscovered in the 1930's and made a cult. Sullivan was apparently unaware that most of his ideas stemmed directly from the indomitable Viollet-le-Duc, and even his ornament can be traced to certain Gothic designs favored by the master. It is part of Sullivan's tragedy that he believed instead that his ideas were the pronouncements of a mysterious inner voice.

Of course, the most important Picturesque Secessionist is Frank Lloyd Wright, and although he is still very much with us he belongs to its first phase. After a year of engineering school, some indoctrination from Viollet-le-Duc and important years under Sullivan, Wright was paddling his own canoe by 1893. From the very beginning he has been a Secessionist, declaring that only he could revive "the Gothic spirit of building" and he rejoiced in Victor Hugo's blast at the Renaissance in the novel *Notre Dame de Paris,* "that setting sun all Europe mistook for dawn." This Gothic child, Gothic in the Viollet-le-Duc sense, worked in the growing suburbs of Chicago, where he planted his "prairie" or bungalow-style house; here he discovered "the decorative value of the plain surface" and texture. He took over the name "organic" to replace "rational," and we can see the "organism" at work in his buildings, which are designed from "within."

Through his furniture he betrays another, lesser link to the inventor of the Morris chair. The famous English craftsman had revived medieval handicrafts much as did the restorer on the other side of the Channel and, like Eastlake, had found American disciples in Gustav Stickley (1858–1942) of mission-style fame and especially Elbert Hubbard (1856–1915), the pioneer advertising man. The latter was a close friend of the youthful Wright. John Lloyd Wright recalls the two of them talking, which they apparently did by the hour: "Said Elbert the Hubbard to the Papa one night 'Modesty being egotism turned wrong side out, let me say here that I am an orator, a great orator! I have health, gesture, imagination, voice, vocabulary, taste, ideas—I acknowledge it myself. What I lack in shape I make up in nerve . . .' Said Dad the Papa to the Hubbard, 'Not only do I intend to be the greatest architect who has yet lived, but the greatest who will ever live. Yes, I intend to be the greatest architect of all time, and I do hereunto affix "the red square" and sign my name to this warning.' " Wright's costume, the flowing tie, the flowing hair, and broad-brimmed pork-pie hat, is that of the advertising man who began his career as a successful soap salesman. So too are his grasp of the value of publicity and his furniture designs. Hubbard made his furniture under the Roycroft label in East Aurora, New York, in the neo-primitive fashion advocated by Morris; Wright's distinctively uncomfortable products take after his. And Wright's curious narcissus cult, carried on in the low hills of Wisconsin and in the Arizona desert under the name of Taliesin Fellowship, is a reflection of the Roycroft Community. (The Fellows are admirers of Wright who are presumably studying to be architects. No one seems to have commented on the absurdity of having an architectural school in a desert and indeed it is one more example of the unreality of the Modernist outlook.)

There were other, less conspicuous Secessionists at this time, only now attracting attention, namely Walter Burley Griffin, William Gray Purcell, George Grant Elmslie, and Dwight H. Perkins of Chicago, Wilson Eyre, Jr., of Philadelphia, and Charles Sumner Greene and his brother, Henry Mather Greene of Pasadena. They, including Wright, were the architectural equivalent of Tiffany's famous favrile glass, an American version of the *art nouveau.* Outside of the suburbs where these men worked Picturesque Secessionism had come to an end in the 1890's; the World's Columbian Exposition was the great blow. When it emerged once again in the 1930's, it would come from Europe rather than from the "prairie."

## 3. THE EUROPEAN INTERLUDE

We have seen how Viollet-le-Duc proved to have more followers in Germany, England, and even for a while in America than among his own countrymen. After his death in 1879 his theories continued to spread slowly abroad. Although there was a flurry over his ideas in the form of the *art nouveau* around 1900 in Paris, a fashion that actually had its origin in Brussels, it was not until the 1920's that his rationalism found a solid support at home.

Holland, Belgium, and Germany were the principal countries which welcomed his ideas in the latter part of the century, and they rewarded his shadow with some surprising specimens of architecture. There is the example of Holland, for instance. Much as in France in the 1850's, the Dutch rediscovered their Gothic monuments and bent every effort to save and restore them. This work fell to Josephus Petrus Hubertus Cuypers (1827–1921), a very able architect, not to be confused with his son, Josephus (1861–1949), an architect in his own right. Known as the Dutch Viollet-le-Duc, the elder Cuypers never lost an opportunity to praise the prophet for his theories, his character, his position in the art world, and his struggle against the Académie and the École. Rationalism in Holland passed from Cuypers to Hendrik Petrus Berlage (1856–1934), architect of the Amsterdam Bourse. Berlage always credited three men for his ideas: Cuypers, Gottfried Semper, of whom more later, and Viollet-le-Duc. He was fond of quoting the last-named to the effect "that all shape which is not regulated by structure should be rejected." From Berlage the Dutch Secessionists have taken their cue.

In Belgium Baron Victor Horta (1861–1947) was the link between the restorer and the *art nouveau* or Paris subway-entrance-style. Although he studied architecture in a traditional atelier, he too acknowledged "his true master." Several houses of his in Brussels marked the first definite attempt of the fashion and inspired its leader, Henry van de Velde (1863–1957).

Henry van de Velde was the most enthusiastic spokesman for the Secessionist approach between 1900 and 1914. Much like Sullivan, the Belgian architect does not credit Viollet-le-Duc for his ideas. Instead he has insisted that Ruskin and William Morris were his gods; like so many, he imbibed the Frenchman's influence unconsciously, largely through Horta's work. His writings, more than his designs, reveal the rationalism. Reviewing his lifework not long ago, he explained that his aim in achieving an original style was always "on the basis of a rational conception of pure forms determined by their function," a statement which would never have fallen from the lips of the two Englishmen. Or if we look at his book, *Amo* (the word familiar to those who have had first-year Latin, meaning "I love"), published in German in Leipzig in 1912, we will see that he laid down three articles of faith:

"You must grasp the form and construction of all objects only in terms of their boldest logic and of their raison d'être.

"You must fit and subordinate these forms and constructions to the essential demand of the material which you use.

"And when you wish to embellish these forms and constructions, you must only carry out this desire in so far as you can respect and keep the truth and the essential appearance of these forms and constructions." We have heard all of this before.

In the 1890's Van de Velde worked in and around Brussels in the manner that came to be called *art nouveau* and also in French "le Moderne Style." The show case for the movement was the Galerie Bing in Paris, where Van de Velde had an exhibition in 1896. His work was seen there by a German Maecenas, one Karl Ernst Osthaus, and on the latter's invitation to come to the city of Hagen to build the Folkwang Museum he moved to Germany. In 1901 he, Peter Behrens, Josef M. Olbrich, and others built Secessionist houses for the Grand Duke Ludwig of Hesse-Darmstadt. In the meantime his ideas were spread by a group of magazines called *Pan, Jugend,* and *Dekorative Kunst* in revolt against the Wilhelmian generation. When he became head of the Kunstgewerbeschule (Technical Arts School) in Weimar, he was the recognized leader of the *"neue Stil."* With the outbreak of war in 1914 Van de Velde as a Belgian had to leave the scene of his triumphs and it was a blow from which he never recovered, for he did little in the remainder of his life. His successor at the Kunstgewerbeschule was none other than Walter Gropius, who changed the name of the institution to the more fitting one of *Bauhaus.*

In Austro-Hungary Viollet-le-Duc's ideas were primarily influential in city planning. Camillo Sitte, next to Baron Haussmann, the most important planner of the century, obtained his conception of picturesque planning from the portion of the *Discourses* describing the medieval city. Head of the Vienna Technical School, he outlined the theory in his well-known *Der Stadtebau nach seinen künstlerischen Grundsätzen* published in 1889. (Professor Steen Eiler Rasmussen of the Royal Academy of Architecture of Copenhagen, visiting professor of city planning at Yale University in 1954, kindly confirmed this point for the author.) In influencing the rational architecture of Vienna, Viollet-le-Duc shared the stage with Gottfried Semper (1803–79). Berlage, we have seen, had pointed to him as one of his teachers, having actually studied under him at the Eidgenossische Polytechnikum in Zurich.

Second to Karl Friedrich Schinkel among the German architects of the nineteenth century, Semper began his education with several years in the ateliers of Paris architects, notably Hittorff. There he acquired a touch of pre-Viollet-le-Duc rationalism, of the Durand, Rondelet, Labrouste variety. His early work, mostly to be found in Dresden, does not reveal the strain, and that includes his justly famous opera house in the Saxon capital. His career there came to an end in 1848 with the revolution, when he fled Saxony along with Richard Wagner. He went to Paris and then to London, where he designed the magnificent funeral car of the Duke of Wellington in 1852, a superb evocation of imperial Rome; it is now in the crypt of St. Paul's. Although tempted at one point to come to this country, he was finally called to head the architectural department of the newly founded Zurich Eidgenossische Polytechnikum. In the course of his wanderings he did some writing which was finally published under the title *Der Stil in den technischen und tektonischen Künsten* (1861–63). In it he offered a rationalist interpretation of ornament, decoration, and architecture, and it enjoyed some influence but never that equal to the works of Viollet-le-Duc, partly because he did not stand on his theories in practice and partly because of his fondness for the Italian Renaissance, anathema to all Picturesque Secessionists. Thanks to the practice he and his sons enjoyed in Vienna, where he later settled, his ideas found a local outlet, although nothing came of them until after his death the same year as that of Viollet-le-Duc.

Suddenly in the 1890's a very successful Viennese architect working the Renaissance manner, named Otto Wagner (1841–1918), declared himself against the classical and for rationalism. In 1893 he entered and won a competition for the planning of several Viennese suburbs, proclaiming as his motto *"Artis sola domina necessitas"* and saying that henceforth he would design only in the *Nutzstil* or "useful style."

Three years later a book appeared, entitled *Moderne Architektur,* the first use of the word "Modern" in the contemporary Secessionist sense. No book at the turn of the century contained as much of the doctrine as did Wagner's. Oddly enough for a leading architect of the Hapsburg Empire he announced functional architecture as the only democratic one, anticipating in this Sullivan's *Kindergarten Chats.* "Every new style has gradually risen from earlier styles because new types of construction, new materials, new human duties and perceptions have called for a change or reconstruction of existing forms . . ." he explained, and he asked that "the art of our time must offer modern forms created by us, which can answer to us, work for us and speak for us."

Accepted as the leader of the *Wiener Sezession,* as it came to be called (note the German use of the word "secession"), he did work which is astonishingly close to that of Wright, only it had more ornament. For some of his fellow-Viennese there was too much ornament, or at least so thought Adolf Loos (1870–1933). This architectural rebel, who worked for a few years in New York in the 1890's as a newspaper reporter, wanted an architecture where "each material had its own form of expression and that no material could assume the forms of another material." He proclaimed that "art has nothing to do with falsification and with lying,"

138

*The interior of St. Jean de Montmartre (1894–1904), by Anatole de Baudot. One of the earliest examples of "functional" church architecture. (A. Papillon, courtesy Liturgical Arts Society)*

meaning that stucco, for example, should never be made to resemble marble or that a building should never have a façade which did not reveal the mechanics of construction. In 1912 he even declared that "the path of culture leads away from the ornamented to the unornamented."

All the main premises of modern Picturesque Secessionism were fixed about forty years ago. In France Antoine de Baudot built the church of St. Jean de Montmartre between 1894 and 1904 following his master's rules. He succeeded in covering the largest space at the lowest possible cost, using reinforced concrete, and in the process he built a church of unparalleled ugliness. Auguste Perret (1874–1954) carried on where de Baudot left off and expressed himself with rational zest in the same material with somewhat better results. (Modern church architecture is generally dated from his Notre Dame de Raincy outside of Paris, completed in 1925.) His earlier works, a few apartment houses, and other Secessionist efforts prior to 1914 were completely overshadowed by such work as the Grand and Petit Palais, the Alexander III Bridge, and the Gare d'Orsay, now being converted into an airline terminal, the last-named being by Victor Laloux, who taught Arthur Brown, Jr., and William Adams Delano.

In England the rising star of Sir Edwin Lutyens eclipsed the heirs of the Pre-Raphaelites. His success helped the Edwardian era turn its back on William Morris, who held, among other opinions, that St. Paul's was the ugliest building in the world, with St. Peter's a close second. Classical Paris was the model for men like Arthur J. Davis, who had as partner the French architect Charles Mewès, and Sir Reginald Blomfield, who had been trained at the École. The Ritz Hotel and the Royal Automobile Club belong to Mewès and Davis, while Blomfield did the Carlton Club. Spain offered much the same picture except in Barcelona, where the chief disciple of Viollet-le-Duc on the south side of the Pyrenees could be found, namely Antonio Gaudí (1852–1926). Of all the Picturesque Secessionists he has produced some of the oddest structures, notably in the Church of the Holy Family and the Casa Bateló. Italy flirted with *art nouveau* in the north, notably at an exposition in Turin, but for Secessionism to gain any roots the Italians had to wait until Mussolini decreed the Modern to be the architectural style of the fascist era, beginning with the Florence Railroad Station in 1935.

*The Casa Bateló (1905–07) in Barcelona, by Antonio Gaudí. An example of Secessionism gone wild which is still taken seriously. (Wayne Andrews)*

After the First World War many individuals who had known only an obscure existence before 1914 now leaped onto the public stage for the first time. Europe, in search of novelty and diversion after four terrible years, found itself more than rewarded. The antics of the Dada amused and horrified; the experimenters at the Bauhaus, heirs to Van de Velde, enjoyed upsetting the burghers of Weimar and later Dessau, where it was to move. Youth had its glorious day in shocking the world. Now that these antics have been codified and made academic, the savor has gone and only a certain sadness remains at the sight of Modernists who, older, continue to take the antics seriously.

To an extent the irrational and the fantastic ruled the postwar revels, but there was far more contriving than we realize. Besides there was a strong rationalist drive represented by the abstract in painting as well as in architecture. It was not odd that a leading Dadaist, the art critic Tristan Tzara, had his Paris house designed by Loos. We must not forget how often the picturesque, resulting from the most thorough structural dialectics, fitted the decade's insistence on the bizarre. The age had taken as its motto that of Viollet-le-Duc: "Be Modern," and Modern they would be. The man who stood foursquare in the middle of the revelry was the man who announced the architectural creed, Le Corbusier (1887–    ). He had mastered the restorer's message when working in Perret's office, from the German Peter Behrens (1868–1940), who had known Van de Velde, and from Loos. Le Corbusier's first house was entirely derived from Loos. After the war the Franco-Swiss became known quite suddenly through his magazine, *L'Esprit nouveau,* edited jointly with Amadée Ozenfant. Here the work of Jean Cocteau nudged an article of Loos; Walt Whitman shared the page with the painter Fernand Léger. Le Corbusier's own articles, written in his admirable "punchy" style, were later assembled in book form in *Vers une architecture* and enjoyed considerable popularity among architects and designers. The English edition of 1927 was a translation from the thirteenth French edition. We now know that the work is a popular simplification of the theories of Viollet-le-Duc where the word "functional" replaces "rational," but the ideas were new to a generation which had forgotten the restorer. It was unquestionably the most decisive architectural book of the generation. The importance given to the plan, the insistence on the new materials, the praise of the mechanical—instead of Viollet-le-Duc's locomotive we have the automobile; instead of his cast iron we have reinforced concrete—were reiterated in twentieth-century terms. And he called for the revolution in architecture which would offset the political and social revolution.

Picturesque Secessionism now raged throughout Europe, especially in France, Germany, and Holland. Perret and Le Corbusier were among the main lights in France, but there were others, mostly the men who had designed for the *Exposition des Arts décoratifs* of 1925. In Germany the aptly named Bauhaus proved a magnet for the German Modernists in all the arts, attracting Paul Klee, Moholy-Nagy, Marcel Breuer, and Theo van Doesberg. The Dutch revolved around the group known as *De Stijl,* which published a magazine of that name. J. J. P. Oud (1890–   ), who had studied under one of the Cuypers and Berlage, built abstract

141

public-housing projects. William Marinus Dudok (1884–    ), who looked to Berlage for inspiration and at times the early work of Wright, also did housing projects and public buildings, his most famous being the city hall of Hilversum. Finland, a new country after 1918, came up with several men, notably Eliel Saarinen (1873–1950), who had known Peter Behrens. His work definitely belongs to the heavier German aspect of Secessionism. Russia was also to know its influence.

Only America was mildly interested because its Renaissance had not yet faded. When the second American phase of the Viollet-le-Duc philosophy came to this country, it was thanks not to Wright but to the Europeans, above all Le Corbusier.

## 4. THE SECOND AMERICAN PHASE

The first impact of the new Secessionism appeared in 1922, when the Chicago *Tribune* held its famous competition for its tower. The winning design of Raymond Hood and John M. Howells, now generally conceded to be the most beautiful sky-scraper in Chicago and one of the most beautiful in the country, did not gain the acclaim of the critics or of many architects. Although each exterior pier masks a steel column, there was too much concession to the decorative, albeit Gothic. Instead the massive design of Eliel Saarinen which had come second, took the critical honors. "It goes freely in advance, and, with the steel frame as a thesis, displays a high science of design . . ." lauded the aging Sullivan. It drew American attention for the first time to the work being done on the other side of the Rhine and influenced the design of the New York Telephone Building by Ralph Walker of McKenzie, Voorhees and Gmelin. The new German rationalists, far more severe than the prewar variety, startled Americans with their plain surfaces, their glass windows, and the cube shapes, as did the Dutch work. At first Americans followed Saarinen and the others by timidly stripping their buildings of ornament, much as a few painters were beginning to strip their pictures of content. If they made use of ornament, they drew on that of the *Exposition des Arts décoratifs,* a lively style which probably achieved its apogee in the interior decoration of French ocean liners of the 1930's. Raymond Hood and John M. Howells turned to it in decorating the entrance and lobby of the New York *Daily News* Building. A third, somewhat obscure, element was that of a number of Germans and Austrians who came to this country directly after 1918; several attained considerable prominence notably Richard M. Schindler (1890–1953), Richard Neutra (1892–    ) and Frederick J. Kiesler (1892–    ), the last two being pupils of Loos.

The crash of 1929 and the depression that followed form a division point in the story of American architecture because the construction industry came to a stop in 1932. When it revived slowly in 1936, the American Renaissance was fight-ing a battle already lost, and the fighting was largely confined to the schools. In domestic architecture the client had all but disappeared. In commercial work the new Secessionism began pushing aside the stripped traditional; only in government work did the classical survive, and then by the end of the decade it knew the stripped. In one branch of government work, public housing, the work was taken

142

*The new City Hall of New Orleans. Completed in 1957 on the designs of Goldstein, Parham & Labouisse and of Favrot, Reed, Mathes & Bergman. An example of the Modern in government work. (Randon Picture Service, courtesy New Orleans Municipality)*

over by the newcomers. Finally the Secessionists had a powerful ally in that extraordinary institution in New York known as the Museum of Modern Art, founded in 1929; the Modern had become chic. With its large body of members, now numbering over twenty-five thousand, with its numerous lavish publications, with its circulating exhibitions and other educational activities, with its large energetic staff, and with the support of generous philanthropists, notably members of the Rockefeller family, it is the strongest single force behind Picturesque Secessionism. When many European Modernists came here late in the 1930's, the country was well prepared to welcome them, for with few exceptions the American Renaissance was dead. The schools went over to Modernism, beginning with that of Columbia University around 1937 and then that of Harvard in 1938. In one after the other it found a foothold, until by the end of the Second World War they had all been converted. Picturesque Secessionism now moved into high gear.

*Secessionist designs compared. A project of the 1900's for a great hall, by Anatole de Baudot, using reinforced concrete.*

What of Wright, who looms so large today? Despite the triumph of the American Renaissance in the 1900's, he was able to pursue his career with considerable success in suburban Chicago. In 1910 a book about his work was published in Berlin and warmly greeted by the members of the *Sezession* in Vienna and functionalists in Holland and Germany. About the same time Wright was not quite as active, although he was soon to be compensated by the spectacular commission of the Imperial Hotel in Tokyo. By the late 1920's he went into total eclipse, hardly eased by the depression that followed.

In spite of his disappearance from the architectural scene he had attracted many defenders, notably Lewis Mumford, who is unquestionably the outstanding American apologist for Secessionism. With the revival of interest in rational architecture in the mid 1930's many of its converts were unhappy at being wholly dependent on Europe for ideas; they wanted an American whose work showed that we could match the Europeans at their game. Wright proved to be the man. Despite the hardships he had suffered he had lost none of his vigor and his spark. An entertaining personality at most times, he swept all others off the architectural platform in the eyes of the public. There is no nonsense of money economy about Wright; one of the interesting aspects of the man is his special genius to persuade the client to spend and spend, much as Viollet-le-Duc could make Napoleon III finance the restoration of some ruined castle. Finally, it is obvious that he had learned his lesson well from Elbert Hubbard, supremely useful in an age when self-promotion is at a premium.

144

*The interior of the Johnson Wax Administration Building (1939), Racine, Wisconsin, also in reinforced concrete, by Frank Lloyd Wright. (Wayne Andrews)*

"Falling Water," the Kaufmann house, opened his second phase, and commissions flowed his way with the increasing publicity which gathered momentum after he was discovered. This time he has gone far beyond the outskirts of Chicago. By the end of the last war he was being offered, and he is still being offered, to the world as our greatest living architect and, what is more, being accepted as such. His boast to Hubbard has been fulfilled. Future generations, enjoying somewhat more perspective in these matters than we, will probably single out others of his generation for honor, namely John Russell Pope, Arthur Brown, Jr., Welles Bosworth, and William Adams Delano.

Wright's way of building, like Louis Sullivan's ornament, has few imitators by contrast to his many admirers. Le Corbusier and, to a lesser degree, Walter Gropius and Ludwig Miës van der Rohe remain the bellwethers of the Secessionists. Among the more successful followers of the first are Wallace K. Harrison and the firm of Skidmore, Owings and Merrill. Gropius can point to Pietro Belluschi and Eero Sa-

*The familiar horizontal Secessionism of today. Oregonian Building (1948) in Portland, Oregon, by Pietro Belluschi, dean of the M.I.T. School of Architecture. (Wayne Andrews)*

arinen as his foster children. In Philip Johnson Miës van der Rohe has his best-known disciple. William Wilson Wurster, head of the architectural school of the University of California, wavers between Wright and Le Corbusier. Most of the work done looks uncommonly alike no matter what drafting board gives it birth.

But there are signs of change in the air. Some of them speak of the "romance of the classical," others have turned to collecting Tiffany's favrile glass, and there is much talk of the *art nouveau*. Incredible as it may seem, Antonio Gaudí has lately been resurrected by the Museum of Modern Art. Edward D. Stone has forsaken glass for the cement grille, which Auguste Perret devised in the 1920's. It is evident that the tide has turned and the Secessionist flood is ebbing along the channel it chose several generations ago. Given time, it will eventually join the classical sea.

# Notes to the Appendix

(Eugène-Emmanuel Viollet-le-Duc is indicated by the letter V.)

For Frank Lloyd Wright and V.,
JOHN LLOYD WRIGHT, *My Father Who Is on Earth* (New York, 1946), pp. 69, 70, 136
Also FRANK LLOYD WRIGHT, *An Autobiography* (New York, 1943), p. 75

The use of the word "organism" by V.,
EUGÈNE-EMMANUEL VIOLLET-LE-DUC, *Entretiens sur l'architecture* (Paris, 1863), Vol. 2, pp. 63, 77

V. on how to use one's reason,
*ibid.,* Vol. 1, p. 176

On Canon de Cordemoy and Abbé Laugier,
LOUIS HAUTECOEUR, *Histoire de l'architecture classique en France* (Paris, 1952), Vol. 4, pp. 50–53

On Canon de Cordemoy,
CHANOINE DE CORDEMOY, *Nouveau traite de toute l'architecture utile aux entrepreneurs, aux ouvriers, et ceux qui font bâtir* (Paris, 1706)

Quotation from Abbé Laugier,
MARC-ANTOINE LAUGIER, *Essai sur l'architecture* (2nd edition, Paris, 1755), p. 34

On the Italian rationalists of the eighteenth century,
HAUTECOEUR, opus cited, Vol. 4, pp. 53–55
Also ANTONIO NAVA, "La teoria di Viollet-le-Duc e l'architettura funzionale," in *La Critica d'arte,* Vol. 8 (1949), pp. 60–65

Laugier's influence on Sir John Soane,
SIR JOHN SOANE, *The Portrait of Sir John Soane, R.A. (1753–1837),* set forth in letters from his friends (1775–1837), edited by Arthur T. Bolton (London, 1927), pp. 142, 143
Also SIR JOHN SOANE, *Lectures on Architecture* edited from the original manuscript by Arthur T. Bolton (London, 1929), p. 5

Geometric shapes of Ledoux,
CLAUDE-NICOLAS LEDOUX, *L'Architecture considérée sous le rapport de l'art, des moeurs et de la législation* (Paris, 1804)

On J. N. L. Durand and Jean-Baptiste Rondelet,
HAUTECOEUR, opus cited, Vol. 5, pp. 259–64, 266

On Hittorff and Labrouste and their interest in rationalism,
ANDRÉ MICHEL, *Histoire de l'art, depuis les premiers temps chretiens jusqu'à nos jours* (Paris, 1925),
   Vol. 8, Part 1, pp. 30, 32
Also HAUTECOEUR, opus cited, Vol. 6, pp. 228–38, 241–47

The influence of Durand, Labrouste, and others on V.,
MICHEL, opus cited, Vol. 8, Part 1, pp. 487–88

Anatole de Baudot and V., and the ateliers of V.,
ANATOLE DE BAUDOT, *L'Architectue. Le Passé. Le Present.* (Paris, 1916), pp. 139, 197–99
Also MICHEL, opus cited, Vol. 8, Part 1, p. 498

The biography of V.,
PAUL GOUT, *Viollet-le-Duc, sa vie, son oeuvre, sa doctrine,* in *Revue de l'Art chrétien,* Supplement 3
   (Paris, 1914)
Also JOHN SUMMERSON, *Heavenly Mansions* (New York, 1949), pp. 135–58

V.'s comments on the École des Beaux Arts,
GOUT, opus cited, pp. 18–19

On the influence of Romantic literature and outlook on architecture.
GEOFFREY SCOTT, *The Architecture of Humanism* (New York, 1956), two chapters devoted to "The
   Romantic Fallacy"

Instruction of Mérimée to V.,
PROSPER MÉRIMÉE, *Lettres à Viollet-le-Duc, 1839–1870* (Paris, 1927), p. 1

V. on restoration,
EUGÈNE-EMMANUEL VIOLLET-LE-DUC, *Dictionnaire raisonné de l'architecture française du XIe au
   XVIe siècle* (Paris, 1868), Vol. 8, p. 14

V. and the imperial court,
MÉRIMÉE, opus cited, pp. 17, 68

V., Bartholdi and the Statue of Liberty,
GOUT, opus cited, p. 62

V. tells Richard Morris Hunt about his illustrations,
CATHERINE HOWLAND HUNT, *Biography of Richard Morris Hunt* (unpublished ms. in the Richard
   Morris Hunt papers, typewritten copy edited by Alan Burnham), p. 97

V. and the number of his illustrations,
CHARLES WETHERED, "The late Eugène-Emmanuel Viollet-le-Duc," Royal Institute of British
   Architects, *Transactions* (session 1883–84), p. 211

V. and his theories,
SUMMERSON, opus cited, pp. 146–50

V. and the function of the pinnacle,
VIOLLET-LE-DUC, *Dictionnaire,* Vol. 7, p. 177

V. and how to attain  an "art of our time,"
VIOLLET-LE-DUC, *Entretiens,* Vol. 2, p. 61

For thorough criticism of V.'s conception of the Gothic,
VICTOR SABOURET, "Les Voutes nervurées, rôle simplement décoratif des nervures," in *Le Génie
   Civil,* March 3, 1928
Also POL ABRAHAM, *Viollet-le-Duc et le rationalisme Médiéval* (Paris, 1934)

V. on the French classical,
VIOLLET-LE-DUC, *Dictionnaire raisonné,* Vol. 1, pp. 165–66

Description of V.'s lectures at the École des Beaux Arts,
*Revue générale de l'architecture et des travaux publics,* Vol. 22 (1864), pp. 67–69
Also *L'Illustration,* Vol. 43 (February 6, 1864), p. 83
Also GOUT, opus cited, p. 52
Also SUMMERSON, opus cited, pp. 142–43
Also MÉRIMÉE, opus cited, pp. 94 (also notes), 97, 98, 100, 102, 106, 108, 109, 114–17
Also for gossip and entertaining description of the lectures and riot, MAXIME DU CAMP, *Souvenirs d'un demi-siècle,* Vol. 1 (Paris, 1949), pp. 217–24

Description of Henry Hobson Richardson and the Beaux Arts riots over V.,
MARION SCHUYLER VAN RENSSELAER, *Henry Hobson Richardson and His Works* (New York, 1888), pp. 15–16

V. and the success of his works in England and Germany,
ANON., "Memorial to Eugène-Emmanuel Viollet-le-Duc," in Royal Institute of British Architects, *Transactions* (session 1879–80), p. 226

For letter of Ungewitter about V.,
AUGUST REICHENSPERGER, *Georg Gottlob Ungewitter und sein Wirken als Baumeister* (Leipzig, 1866), pp. 152, 186

On Street, Morris, and the English in the Lille Cathedral Competition,
ARTHUR EDMUND STREET, *Memoir of George Edmund Street, R.A., 1824–1881* (London, 1888), pp. 24–29

On Street and his admiration of V.,
GEORGE EDMUND STREET, *Unpublished Notes and Reprinted Papers,* with an essay by Georgiana Goddard King (New York, 1916), p. 162

V. and England,
CHARLES LOCKE EASTLAKE, *A History of the Gothic Revival* (London, 1872), pp. 317, 318

Eastlake and the rationalist point of view,
CHARLES LOCKE EASTLAKE, *Hints on Household Taste in Furniture, Upholstery and Other Details* (Boston, 1872), pp. 36, 172

Henry van Brunt on V.'s approach to the Gothic,
EUGENE-EMMANUEL VIOLLET-LE-DUC, *Discourses on Architecture,* translated with introduction by Henry van Brunt (Boston, 1875), pp. IX, X

Ruskin's comment on the *Dictionnaire raisonné,*
SIR SIDNEY CARLYLE COCKERELL, *Friends of a Lifetime; Letters to Sydney Carlyle Cockerell,* edited by Viola Meynell (London, 1940), p. 54

Richard Morris Hunt and V.'s ideas,
J.A.S., "A Reminiscence and an Appreciation," in *The Architectural Record,* Vol. 39 (March, 1916), pp. 295–97
Also PETER B. WIGHT, "Richard Morris Hunt," in *The Inland Architect and News Record,* Vol. 26 (1895), pp. 3, 4

Eugène Millet on Labrouste and V.,
DE BAUDOT, opus cited, p. 199

Taine on St. Peter's in Rome,
HIPPOLYTE TAINE, *Voyage en Italie* (Paris, 1866), Vol. 1, p. 27

On Hunt's atelier in the 1850's and 1860's,
CATHERINE HOWLAND HUNT, opus cited, pp. 43–57

Richard Morris Hunt calls on V.,
CATHERINE HOWLAND HUNT, opus cited, *ibid.,* p. 138

V., influence on Henry Hobson Richardson,
LEWIS MUMFORD, *Sticks and Stones* (New York, 1924), p. 101

Career of Louis Sullivan,
WAYNE ANDREWS, *Architecture, Ambition and Americans* (New York, 1955), pp. 213–20

On the design of the Wainwright Building, St. Louis,
IRVING K. POND, "Louis Sullivan's 'The Autobiography of an Idea,'" in *Western Architecture,*
   Vol. 33 (1924), p. 69

Frank Lloyd Wright and Elbert Hubbard,
JOHN LLOYD WRIGHT, opus cited, pp. 32, 33

P. J. H. Cuypers' admiration of V.,
*Het Werk van Dr. P. J. H. Cuypers, 1827–1917* (Amsterdam, 1917), pp. 34, 35
Also "PETRUS JOSEPHUS HUBERTUS CUYPERS," in *Winkler Prins Encyclopaedie* (Amsterdam, Brussels, 1949), Vol. 6, p. 578

Berlage on Semper and V.,
*Dr. H. P. Berlage en zijn werk door K.P.C. de Bazel . . .* (Rotterdam, 1916), p. 3
Also *Dr. H. P. Berlage Bouwmeester, 230 afbeeldingen van zijn werk met een inleiding door Ir. Jan
   Gratama* (Rotterdam, 1928), p. xv

Berlage quotes V.,
H. P. BERLAGE, *De Ontwikkeling der moderne Bouwkunst in Holland* (Amsterdam, 1925), p. 13

Baron Victor Horta and V.,
CHARLES CONRARDY, "L'Oeuvre de Victor Horta," in *Architecture. Urbanisme. Habitation* (1948),
   p. 84

Quotation from Henry van de Velde,
HENRY VAN DE VELDE, *Amo* (Leipzig, 1912), pp. 10, 11

Van de Velde on his work,
HENRY VAN DE VELDE, "Les premières tentatives pour le relèvement du niveau esthetique . . .,"
   in *Werk* Vol. 35 (February 1948), No. 2, pp. 36–40

Van de Velde in Germany,
GUSTAV ADOLF PLATZ, *Die Baukunst der neuesten Zeit,* (2nd edition, Berlin, 1930), Vol. 1, pp 26–29

On Gottfried Semper and his ideas,
HANS SEMPER, *Gottfried Semper: Ein Bild seiner Lebens und Wirkens...* (Berlin, 1880), pp. 3, 4, 21

Otto Wagner and the *Nutzstil,*
THIEME-BECKER, *Künstler-Lexikon* (Leipzig, 1942), Vol. 35, pp. 46, 47

Otto Wagner on the new style,
OTTO WAGNER, *Die Baukunst unserer Zeit* (4th edition, Vienna, 1914), pp. 31, 33

For Adolf Loos,
*Adolf Loos, Das Werk des Architekten,* edited by Heinrich Kulka (Vienna, 1931), pp. 19, 22
Also ADOLF LOOS, *Trotzdem, 1900–1930* (Innsbruck, 1931)

De Baudot and St. Jean de Montmartre,
MICHEL, opus cited, Vol. 8, Part 2, p. 498

On Arthur J. Davis, Sir Reginald Blomfield, and other classical English architects of this century,
CHARLES HERBERT REILLY, *Representative British Architects of the Present Day* (London, 1931),
pp. 54–62, 67–79

On Gaudí and V.,
J. F. RAFOLS, *Gaudí, 1852–1926* (3rd edition, Barcelona, 1952), p. 25

Influence of Eliel Saarinen on American architecture,
HENRY-RUSSELL HITCHCOCK, JR., *Modern Architecture, Romanticism, and Reintegration* (New
York, 1929), pp. 148, 200

For the last portion of the Appendix the author has turned to the standard works by leading
Picturesque Secessionists, namely WALTER CURT BEHRENDT, *Modern Building: Its Nature, Prob-
lems, and Forms* (New York, 1937)
HENRY-RUSSELL HITCHCOCK, JR., AND PHILIP C. JOHNSON, *The International Style: Architecture
Since 1922* (New York, 1932)
LEWIS MUMFORD, editor, *Roots of Contemporary American Architecture* (New York, 1952)
NIKOLAUS PEVSNER, *Pioneers of Modern Design from William Morris to Walter Gropius* (2nd
edition, New York, 1949)
J. M. RICHARDS, *An Introduction to Modern Architecture* (London, 1956)

# Further Reading

LEON BATTISTA ALBERTI, *Ten Books of Architecture,* translated into Italian by Cosimo Bartoli and
into English by James Leoni, edited by Joseph Rykwert (Transatlantic Arts, Hollywood-by-
the-Sea, Florida, 1955)
Vitruvius paraphrased by a great Renaissance architect and humanist. Book VI is particularly
valuable.

ROBERT H. IVES GAMMELL, *Twilight of Painting: An Analysis of Recent Trends to Serve in a Period
of Reconstruction* (G. P. Putnam's Sons, New York, 1946)
As the schools have failed to carry on the traditional methods in teaching painting, the author
advocates the return to the apprentice method of the classical, where the artist was trained in the
master's studio.

KATHERINE GILBERT, *Aesthetic Studies: Architecture and Poetry* (Duke University Press, Durham,
North Carolina, 1952)
The late Professor Gilbert offers a devastating study of the Secessionist vocabulary and inter-
prets the Modern movement as mystic nihilism.

TALBOT FAULKNER HAMLIN, *The American Spirit in Architecture* (Yale University Press, New
Haven, 1926)
Although over thirty years old, it remains the only adequate survey of American architecture.
The author makes use of the word "secession" to describe the work of Frank Lloyd Wright.

LOUIS HAUTECOUER, *L'Histoire de l'Architecture classique en France* (Editions A. et J. Picard, Paris, 1943–57), 8 vols.

An invaluable study of the classical in France. Among other particulars the author guides the reader through the "rationalist" architectural theories which have come to a climax in Picturesque Secessionism. It is well indexed, extensively illustrated, and carefully broken up according to subject matter.

WERNER HEGEMAN and ELBERT PEETS, *The American Vitruvius: An Architect's Handbook of Civic Art* (Architectural Book Publishing Company, New York, 1922), Vol. 1

Both for text and for illustrations this is an essential volume for understanding civic art. The reader will find in it most of the great compositions of the American Renaissance as well as those of other eras and nations.

PAUL LANDOWSKI, *Peut-on enseigner les beaux arts?* (Paris, 1944)

A traditional sculptor discusses the problem of instruction in his art.

JACQUES MAROGER, *The Secret Formulas and Techniques of the Masters* (The Studio Publications, Inc., New York and London, 1948)

The author heads the only school of classical painting in America.

FRANZ SALES MEYER, *Handbook of Ornament* (Dover Publications, New York, 1957)

A handy book of ornament available in a paper-back edition.

ALBERT E. RICHARDSON, *Monumental Classic Architecture in Great Britain and Ireland during the Eighteenth and Nineteenth Centuries* (Charles Scribner's Sons, New York, 1914)

The former president of the Royal Academy is a strong proponent of the classical. In this volume he tells of some of the English and Irish triumphs.

GISELA M. A. RICHTER, *The Sculpture and Sculptors of the Greeks* (new revised edition, Yale University Press, New Haven, 1950)

The authority on Greek sculpture reveals its splendor and offers an object lesson in what can be achieved in the art.

GEORGE SANTAYANA, *The Life of Reason: Or the Phases of Human Progress. Vol. IV: Reason in Art* (Charles Scribner's Sons, New York, 1905)

A humanist philosopher looks at beauty and art and points the way to the classical.

MARGARET ROSEMAN SCHERER, *Marvels of Ancient Rome,* edited and with a foreword by Charles Rufus Morey (Phaidon Press, New York, 1955)

The vision of ancient Rome has held multitudes spellbound, not least the American. This is by far the best introduction to a monumental subject.

GEOFFREY SCOTT, *The Architecture of Humanism* (Doubleday & Co., Anchor Books, New York, 1956)

The most important book of the century on architecture written from the classical point of view. In a paper-back edition.

HANS SEDLMAYR, *The Lost Center* (Henry Regnery Company, Chicago, 1958)

Barring certain weaknesses, this is the best history of Modern art in English; it reveals the Modernist fallacies in detail.

HANS SEDLMAYR, *Die Revolution der modernen Kunst* (Rowohlt Taschenbuch Verlag, Hamburg, 1955)

An outright condemnation of the Modernist position in literature and art.

SIR GEORGE SITWELL, *On the Making of Gardens,* with an introduction by Sir Osbert Sitwell (Charles Scribner's Sons, New York, 1951)

A spirited defense of the classical garden.

JOHN SUMMERSON, *Heavenly Mansions* (Charles Scribner's Sons, New York, 1949)
The Secessionist author was the first in recent times to show the importance of Viollet-le-Duc and his part in shaping the Modern.

CHRISTOPHER TUNNARD, *The City of Man* (Charles Scribner's Sons, New York, 1953)
A key volume in the resurgence of the classical, it is a forthright espousal of beauty's role in the community.

CHRISTOPHER TUNNARD and HENRY HOPE REED, *American Skyline* (Houghton Mifflin Company, Boston, 1955, and New American Library of World Literature, Mentor edition, New York, 1956)
A survey of the forces which have shaped the American town and city, one of them being the classical.

PAUL VALERY, "Préambules," in *Pièces sur l'art* (Gallimard, Paris, 1936)
The great French poet offers the classical approach to painting.

VITRUVIUS POLLIO, *The Ten Books on Architecture,* translated by M. H. Morgan (Harvard University Press, Cambridge, 1914)

WLADIMIR WEIDLÉ, *Les abeilles d'Aristée. Essai sur le destin actuel des lettres et des arts* (Librairie Gallimard, Paris, 1954)
A vivid erudite study of the chaos, and its causes, of contemporary literature and art. If it has one main fault, and this is also true of the work of Hans Sedlmayr cited above, it is the neglect of our Graeco-Roman heritage.

EDITH WHARTON and OGDEN CODMAN, JR., *The Decoration of Houses* (Chas. Scribner's Sons, 2nd Edition, New York, 1907)
One of America's great writers joined with a distinguished architect to write the standard work on interior decoration.


*WORKING MANUALS OF THE CLASSICAL:*

JACQUES FRANCOIS BLONDEL, *L'Architecture française* . . . (reprint of 1752–56 edition, Paris, 1904–5), 5 vols.

GUSTAVE CLAUSSE, *Les San Gallo, architectes, peintres, sculpteurs, médailleurs, XVe et XVIe siècles* (Paris, 1900–2), 3 vols.

FRÉDÉRIC CONTET, *Les vieux hotels de Paris* (Paris, 1908–34), 21 vols.

Same author, *Documents du ferronerie ancienne* (Paris, 1908–29), 7 vols.

COLEN CAMPBELL, *Vitruvius Britannicus* (London, 1715–25).

HECTOR D'ESPOUY, *Fragments d'architecture antique d'après les relevés et restaurations des anciens pensionnaires de l'Academie de France à Rome* (Paris, 1905), 2 vols.

Same author, *Fragments d' architecture du Moyen Age et de la Renaissance d'après les relevés des anciens pensionnaires de l'Academie de France à Rome* (Paris, 1910–12), 3 vols.

Same author, *Monuments antiques relevés et restaurés par les architectes pensionnaires de l'Academie de France à Rome* (Paris, 1910–12), 3 vols.

GEORGES GROMORT, *Plans de grandes compositions exécutées* (3rd edition, Vincent Fréal, 1944).

INIGO JONES, *The Designs of Inigo Jones, consisting of plans and elevations for public and private buildings published by William Kent* (London, 1727), 2 vols.

PAUL MARIE LÉTAROUILLY, *Édifices de Rome moderne* (Paris, 1840–68), 4 vols.

*A Monograph of the Work of McKim, Mead & White,* (Architectural Book Publishing Co., New York, 1915), 4 vols.

*Palast-Architektur in Ober-Italien und Toscana vom XIII. bis XVIII. Jahrhundert* (Berlin, 1886–1922), 6 vols.

*The Architecture of Andrea Palladio,* published by James Leoni (London, 1715–20), 5 vols.

PIERRE PATTE, *Monuments érigés en France à la gloire de Louis XV* (Paris, 1767)

GIOVANNI BATTISTA PIRANESI, *Le antichità romane* (Rome, 1748), 4 vols.

R. P. SPIERS, *The Orders of Architecture* (B. T. Batsford, London, 1926)

WILLIAM R. WARE, *The American Vignola* (International Textbook Co., Scranton, Pennsylvania, 1913), Parts 1 and 2

This is a scattered list of useful books for those interested. For detailed bibliographies the reader should turn to the chapter endings of Sir Banister Fletcher's *A History of Architecture on the Comparative Method,* published by Charles Scribner's Sons.

# Glossary of Architectural Terms

| | |
|---|---|
| ACANTHUS | A prickly herb of the Mediterranean region with a leaf that set a pattern for an ornament such as found in the Corinthian capital. |
| ANTEFIXAE | Ornaments set at intervals along the eaves of a roof to conceal the ends of tile joints. |
| BEZANT | A flat disk which takes its name from the coin of the Byzantine Empire. |
| BRACKET | A projecting device to support a weight, it often has the form of a scroll or volute. |
| BUCRANE | An ox skull. |
| CINQUEFOIL | A form of decorative design named after a kind of rose, consisting of five openings with five cusps. |
| CORNICE | The crowning projection of a façade or wall. |
| COURSING OR STRING COURSE | A plain or molded band running horizontally on a wall. |
| CROSSETTES | A form of decoration achieved when the lintel of a doorway is so long as to overrun the doorposts and form projections. |
| CUSP | A pointed end formed by converging curves. |
| ENTABLATURE | The upper part of a wall, often supported by columns or pilasters. It consists of an architrave, cornice, and frieze. |
| GODROON | An ornament made by notching. |
| IMBRICATION | A decoration suggestive of overlapping leaves. |
| KEYSTONE | The central stone of an arch. |
| MULLION | A thin vertical bar between the lights of a window. |
| PILASTER | An upright rectangular projection from a wall, treated architecturally as a column with capital, shaft, and base. |
| QUOIN | Cornerstones found in the angles of buildings to provide added support, often only an ornamental device. |
| RINCEAU | A branching foliated scroll on occasion enriched by acanthus leaves, rosettes, cherubs, and griffons. |
| ROSETTE | An imitation, often very elaborate, of a rose in stone or wood. |
| RUSTICATION, TO RUSTICATE | To recess joints of stonework in order to make them conspicuous. |
| SIGNUM | A Roman standard which holds a banner or wreath. |
| SPANDREL | The triangular space formed by the curves of two contiguous arches and a horizontal line above them. |
| SWAG | A mass of fruit or flowers seemingly woven together to form a rope, sagging between two supports. |
| TORUS | A round molding frequently found in the bases of columns. |
| VERMICULATION | A form of stone surface which resembles worm tracks. |
| VITRUVIAN SCROLL | A wavelike flat ornament. |
| VOLUTE | A scroll of spiral ornament which had its source in the Ionic capital. |
| VOUSSOIRS | The wedge-shaped blocks which form an arch. |

155

# Index

157

Guggenheim Museum, New York City, 15 *illus.,* 58

Harlem housing plan, 102, 104 *illus.,* 105
Harmony, 60, 114
Harral-Wheeler house, 70
Harrison, Peter, 66
Harrison, Wallace K., 37, 45, 58, 145
Harrison & Abromovitz, 33
Harvard University, 143
Hastings, Thomas, 38, 44, 76, 113
Hawthorne, Nathaniel, 49, 60
Hearst Castle, San Simeon, 87
*Heavenly Mansions,* 121
Helleu, Paul, 55
Hewitt Brothers, 132
Hilversum City Hall, Finland, 142
Hittorff, Jacques-Ignace, 124, 138
Hoban, James, 68
Hoffman, F. Burrall, 87
Hohenberg, Johann Ferdinand von, 59
Hood, Raymond, 142
Hooker, Philip, 68
Horta, Victor, 136, 137
*House of the Seven Gables,* 49, 60
Housing projects, failure of, 102
Howells, John M., 142
Hubbard, Elbert, 135, 144–45
Hugo, Victor, 135
Human form, 113, 114
Hunt, Mrs. Jonathan, 74–75
Hunt, Richard Howland, 14
Hunt, Richard Morris, 14, 74, 75, 77, 78, 85, 128, 131–32
Hunt, William Morris, 48, 75

Iconography, 109, 112
Imperial Hotel, Tokyo, 144
Impermanence, 51
Ingres, Jean A., 113, 129
Institut de France, Académie des Beaux Arts, 98, 129, 136
Interdepartmental Auditorium, Washington, D.C., 95 *illus.*
Internal Revenue Building, Washington, D.C., 97, 107

Jackson statues: New Orleans, 73; Washington, D.C., 72, 73 *illus.*
James, Henry, 119
James, William, 101, 119
Jefferson, Thomas, 63, 64, 66, 76, 100, 101, 106, 107, 113, 118
Jefferson Memorial Park Arch, St. Louis, 27, 53

Johnson, Philip C., 35, 39, 146
Johnson Wax Administrative Building, Racine, Wis., interior, 145 *illus.*

Kahn, Louis I., 21, 52
Kaufmann, Edgar K., 31
Kaufmann, house, 31 *illus.,* 56, 57, 145. *See also* "Falling Water"
Kelham, George W., 101
Keisler, Frederick J., 142
King, Frederick Rhinelander, 30, 56, 57, 88
Klee, Paul, 141
Koch, Richard, 90, 91

Labrouste, Henri, 124, 131
Laloux, Victor, 92, 98, 140
Lampposts, 16, *illus.,* 52, 56, 80, 116
Landscape architecture, 115, 116
Lansburgh, G. Albert, 92, 93
Laramie (Wyo.), post office, 79 *illus.*
Latrobe, Benjamin, 68, 69, 72
Laugier, Marc-Antoine, 123
Le Corbusier (C. E. Jeanneret), 54, 58, 141, 145, 146
Ledoux, Claude-Nicholas, 123
Lefuel, Victor, 75
Léger, Fernand, 141
L'Enfant, Pierre Charles, 63, 68, 100
Lescaze, William, 29
Lever House, New York City, 25 *illus.,* 53, 57, 58
Levi, Julian Clarence, 34
Lodoli, Carlo, 123
Loos, Adolf, 138–39, 141, 142
Louvre, Paris, 75, 98; Gallery of Apollo, 119
Lowell, James Russell, 48
Lutyens, Edwin, 140

MacMonnies, Frederick, 26, 76
McKim, Charles Follen, 50, 74, 76, 83, 87, 113, 132
McKim, Mead & White, 50, 74, 77, 98
Manhattan Bridge, New York City, 80
Manufacturers Trust Co.; Brooklyn Heights, 22 *illus.;* Fifth Avenue, 23 *illus.,* 53, 57
Martiny, Philip, 26
Massachusetts Institute of Technology, architecture school, 75, 133, 146
Matsui, Yasuo, 28
Mauriac, François, 58
Maybeck, Bernard, 92
Medary, Milton B., 98
Mellon, Andrew W., 97
Menconi, Raffaele J., 38, 76
Mérimée, Prosper, 125, 126, 127, 129

Metropolitan Museum of Art, New York City, 14

Metropolitan Opera, New York City, 109

Mewès, Charles, 140

Michelangelo, 48, 113

Mies van der Rohe, Ludwig, 39, 145, 146

Modern, 13, 51, 114, 118, 121, 140; aim of, 46–47; characteristics of, 49; elements of, 51–53; Exposition of 1893, 78; fear of past, 48–49, 51, 61; first use of word, 138; and human figure, 113; materials of, 53; ornaments, 83; in U.S. universities, 143; vocabulary of, 53–54. *See also* Picturesque Secessionism; Secessionism

*Modern Architektur,* 138

Morris, Benjamin Wistar, 44, 85

Morris, William, 130, 135, 137, 140

Mount Vernon, 65 *illus.,* 66

Mumford, Lewis, 144

Mural work, 72, 85

Musée d'Art Moderne, Paris, 130

Museum of Modern Art, New York City, 143 146; Guest House, 35 *illus.,* 57

*My Father Who Is on Earth,* 121

Nadelman, Eli, 28, 56

National Gallery of Art, Washington, D.C., 87, 88 *illus.,* 107

National Grand Opera, Washington, D.C., 108, 111

National Repertory Theater, Washington, D.C., 105–6, 112

Neo-Gothic, 70, 131

Neutra, Richard, 142

"New Brutality, The," 57

New Orleans: City Hall, 143 *illus.;* Custom House, 71 *illus.*

New York, N. Y.: City Hall, 68; Coliseum, 109; *Daily News* Building, 142; Port Authority Bus Terminal, 19 *illus.,* 52–53, 55;Park Avenue, 114; proposed Opera House, 108; Stock Exchange, 36 *illus.,* Telephone Building, 142

New York Central Building, 82, 83, 92, 113, 114

Nihilism, 60

Notre Dame, Paris, 121, 135

*Nutzstil,* 138

Olbrich, Josef M., 137

Olmsted, F. L., 83, 116

Oregonian Building, Portland, 146 *illus.*

Organic architecture, 58, 121, 123

Originality, 46–47, 51, 55, 57, 60, 62, 63, 66, 80, 129

Ornaments, 48, 49, 51, 55, 114, 115, 124, 134, 138; absence of, 13, 142; classical, 66; denial of, 60; Gothic, 84 *illus.,* organic, 135; purpose of, 61, 112

Osthaus, Karl Ernst, 137

Oud, J. J. P., 141

Ozenfaut, Amadée, 141

Painting, 55, 113, 117, 130, 141

Palladio's Teatro Olimpico, Vincenza, 107, 108 *illus.*

Park Avenue, New York City, 114

Parthenon, Athens, 120

Patronage, 118, 120

Pennsylvania Avenue, Washington, D.C., 106, 107 *illus.*

Pennsylvania Station, New York City, 83, 99, 113; Great Hall, 50 *illus.*

Permanence, 60, 113

Perret, Auguste, 53, 139, 141, 146

Picturesque Secessionism, 55, 60, 87, 133 *illus.;* characteristics of, 113; in Europe, 136–42; origin of, 121–28; self-destruction of, 91; in U.S.A., 130–36, 142–46. *See also* Modern; Seccessionism

Platt, Charles Adams, 42, 86, 88

Platt, Geoffrey, 88, 89

Platt, William, 88, 89

Pointed Style, 130. *See also* Gothic architecture

Pope, John Russell, 87, 95, 98, 145

Post, George B., 36, 76, 132

Post Office Building, Washington, D.C., façade, 96 *illus.*

Pragmatism, 101

"Prarie" house, 135

Public buildings, 115, 116; ornaments, lack of, 118

Public housing, 142

Public places: absence of, 105; importance, 101

Purism, 54

Rational architecture, 123, 128, 144

"Rationalism," 77, 124, 125, 136, 137, 138; in Austro-Hungary, 137, 138; in Belgium, 136; in England, 140; in France, 134, 139; in Germany, 137, 142; in Holland, 136; in Italy, 140; in Spain, 140. *See also* Modern, Picturesque Secessionism, Secessionism

Rationalist theory, 130, 131

Rea, Samuel, 99

Renaissance, 114, 135; French, 74; Italian, 72, 74, 138